Warm Beer and Iron Ore Dust:
a memoir

By Tom Intihar

Dedicated to R. John and Shirley Intihar, Margaret (Peg) Intihar Lawrence, my wife Traci, and my daughters Jamie, Jenna, and Lauren

Thank you for being my family……..

~Tom Intihar, 2023

Thanks also to Ed Weir, Ray Newman, and Ray Reigstad, whose books inspired this one.

And lastly, everyone who has ever called Eveleth their home. Memories last a lifetime.

"People in small towns, much more than in cities, share a destiny."

~ Richard Russo

Prologue

I'm not sure what possessed me to start this book that I've worked on for more than a few years. It takes different things to think about events that happened more than 40 years ago. It might be telling an Eveleth story to someone and thinking that it might be something to think about and write. It might be a dream. It might be getting together with Eveleth friends I see occasionally like Figgy Ritacco, Mike Hallstrom, David Diggerness, and the Tusa twins Keith and Kevan. It could be a lot of things.

I'm pretty sure I remember the defining moment. It was about eight years ago. My wife Traci and I were going to Minneapolis to do some Christmas shopping. Our three girls found a nice deal on Groupon for a hotel stay downtown and booked it for us. We were not in the habit of leaving the girls overnight just yet. Jamie was 17 and Jenna and Lauren were 13.

Could they handle themselves alone quite well, but overnight? We were not sure if they'd fill the house with friends or be afraid of being alone. We live in Brooklyn Park and there is quite a bit of crime in our city but we decided they could handle it. We also were wondering why they wanted to get rid of us on a Friday night. We had dinner at Ike's Cocktails in downtown Minneapolis. I had texted Figgy Ritacco to see if he was at the restaurant he managed then, The Mission American Kitchen. He was working so we made plans to stop to see him, have a drink, and try to fit in some shopping at Macy's which was open until 10pm during the holiday season.

No sooner did our drinks at Ike's come and Figgy walks in to see us. The Mission was just a half block away from Ike's. Figgy told us some Eveleth natives were at Murray's Steakhouse and to stop after dinner. We agreed.

We arrived at Murray's and saw that Cammy Newman and some classmates were there. We sat at the bar and ordered a drink. I was a couple of sips into my cocktail when a well-dressed gentleman took the seat next to me. He didn't recognize me but I knew exactly who *he* was. It was the legend Jerry Bayuk, all decked out in dapper suit and hat. I introduced myself and we started chatting. I knew

Jerry well when I was a kid running around the bars my dad worked at then and knew all the guys who we saw in downtown Eveleth.

Jerry kept my drink full for a few hours and told many great stories about Eveleth in the 1960's and 70's. It was interesting and educational for me and we had a lot of laughs. I told Jerry that he should write a book as he had a ton of good material.

Needless to say, Traci and I never did get to Macy's that night. We closed down the bar with Jerry and Cammy and her friends. It was awesome. We attempted a short shopping time in the morning but we were a bit hungover so we were home by noon and napping. I thought quite a bit about Jerry's stories and thought I could maybe pull together something. I just needed to start.

Several years ago, I found out that Eveleth native Ray Reigstad had written a few books, some of them memoirs. One was called "Truer Than Strange" and was about Eveleth. The other was about his time as a cab driver in Minneapolis, which he referred to as "Mini Apple." Both were very interesting. I love memoirs as a genre. They are basically autobiographies for regular people. I've read many and find that they are as interesting as any biography of a famous person, especially if you could have a connection with the subject or author.

    Eveleth native Ray Newman also wrote a memoir about Eveleth which my parents and I read a couple of times. I liked the format of both books: One story as a chapter, regardless of length. I also thought it could be more of a project that I could work on whenever I had new material.

    Another great read was the memoir of Virginia's Ed Weir, the late husband of my friend Joni (Falkowski) Weir of Virginia. Ed wrote a very moving book about his struggles with ALS in the 1990's. Thanks to all three men for the motivation to get me started on this book.

Introduction

Somewhere about 55 miles north of Duluth on state highway 53, there it is...On this spot looking north, you can see it. Just for a few brief seconds. You need to know when and where to look. If your timing is right and you're looking over the horizon of trees, you can see it. A water tower! This water tower, painted maroon and gold, sits at the highest point of Eveleth, Minnesota.

Eveleth. The name doesn't tell you much. It's just a name. But to be an Evelethian...that's a whole different thing.

How would one describe an Evelethian? Hard working? Yes. Honest? For sure. Helpful? Always. If you're an Evelethian, you have warm beer in your veins and iron ore dust in your throat. And you like it that way!

An Evelethian is always ready to help with any project. They love to work. Ask an Evelethian to give you an hour of help, they'll give you five and never complain. Ever. Complaining is for wimps from the Twin Cities. Or Virginia!

Most native Evelethians are descendants of the immigrant men who blasted iron ore out of underground caves and used picks and axes to break it down and haul it away. They'd work 12 hour shifts for a dollar or two a day and they weren't even the toughest ones in their families. The Eveleth women were. They took care of large broods of children, cleaned homes, cooked meals, dished out punishment, and took absolutely no crap from their kids. I'd bet many who read this would consider their mothers tougher than their fathers. I know I do. My dad is a former US Marine and he toes the line when my mom, Shirley, is around. Thinking about some of the moms I knew like my aunts MaryAnn Mayasich and Annette Kochevar, and my friends' moms, we knew their word was gospel and they raised us with an iron hand and we learned how to treat others with respect and our moms terrified us. Anytime I got in trouble, I feared what my mother would do to me and even, to this day, I listen to her always and respect her opinion.

There is so much to say about the roots we plant in our hometown. These roots never die. In fact, they grow stronger and deeper as we age. It's who we are. I suppose we are no different than anyone else in that respect.

I'm a fan of Bruce Springsteen. When you listen to his songs, especially the early ones, you can experience life as a kid who grew up on the New Jersey shore. I've never been there but the words take you there and you feel like you have. My favorite Iron Ranger, Bob Dylan, did the same with Hibbing, although he left home at 18 and never really returned other than to visit family. Many would say he turned his back on the Range, but do we ever? His songs *Girl from the North Country* and *North Country Blues* tell his and others' Iron Range stories very clearly and although many words and sayings in other songs are imbedded deeper, they show his appreciation for his roots. Remember, many leave the Range, but the Range never really leaves us.

If a former Evelethian or Iron Ranger leaves the Range, they quickly gain an appreciation for the good people of St. Louis County. I've lived in the Twin Cities for 32 years (as of this writing) and let me tell you, things are not always as good as they are

"Up North." People, on the whole, are not as hardworking, trustworthy, helpful, nor do all of them have that Iron Range work ethic that we take for granted.

If you want to appreciate your roots as a person from Eveleth, leave for a number of years. Things are not always as good. Sure, there are many Iron Range-like folks everywhere and many do embody that Iron Range mentality. It's just that not everyone is that way. I find myself really lucky to have these roots but just as lucky to have met friends and work colleagues who demonstrate those Range qualities we love.

When I decided to put these thoughts and stories down, I realized that I had a ton of good material to record. I began making notes in my cell phone so as not to forget the good ones. One of my third-grade students in Champlin told another teacher that my stories about my high school buddies were one of the best reasons to be in my class! So, I figured I had a good idea. Hopefully, you'll think so too.

The pages that follow contain some of my best memories and stories about the greatest people and the greatest small town I've ever known. At least this is how I remember it………

I apologize for the randomness of the book. I wrote the chapters as I remembered them with no clue as to chronological order and clearly, I've never done this before. Enjoy.

1. Beginnings

My great grandfather, John Boben, immigrated from Slovenia. He worked in the iron ore mines and also took in borders: Young, single miners, to make extra cash. He lived in Aurora and was well known to the local policemen. He was arrested and fined on more than one occasion for "running a disorderly house." I have a remake of an article from December,1913, in which he was arrested for owning the home in which there was a stabbing.

My other great grandfathers, Pete Malesh, John Hobyan, and Joseph Intihar, also immigrated from Slovenia. Pete and John were miners and Joseph was a stonemason, a craft learned in Slovenia. He taught the craft to my grandfather

Rudy, who built many fireplaces and chimneys in Eveleth.

If you're keeping score, that makes me a full-blooded Slovenian. For years I've had to explain to people who ask me the origin of my last name. I'd mention Slovenia and was met mostly with blank expressions. It's much easier now that we've learned a bit about former First Lady Melania Trump and as she's a native of Slovenia, there is much more focus on that region.

My grandparents, Mary Boben and Rudy and Mary Intihar, were born and raised in Eveleth. My grandfather, Tony Boben, was born in Pennsylvania and raised in Aurora. Tony's father, my great grandfather John, worked in the steel mills in Pennsylvania which used Iron Range mined iron ore pellets to produce steel. The way I understand the story is that John talked with other Slovenian men who worked on the iron ore trains and found out he could make more money as a miner in northeastern Minnesota so he took his family and young son Tony (his oldest child) and headed to Aurora. I think this was around 1910 or so. Tony was born in 1907.

My grandfathers were miners and at the breakout of World War II, were exempt from being drafted due to the importance of the mining to provide the iron ore to make the steel that was so important to the war effort. They were a bit older at the time so the initial draft would probably not have affected them.

Grandma Mary Intihar worked at the shirt factory for a time before raising her children. She was quite the cook. She could put together a meal for 20 people like it was the easiest thing. I can still hear her laugh.

The best story about her: One time after my dad got out of the Marine Corps, he was living back at home. Home was now an old barn where Grandpa Rudy kept his masonry tools which was converted into a two-floor dwelling with an apartment upstairs and bedroom/laundry room below. When Dad was out on the town, he used to crawl in through a window to sneak back in. He kept the bed below the window and used to just fall into it...a drop of several feet from the window. Being a basement room, it was dark. He thought he was so smart. But Grandma was smarter. She moved the bed one night when he was out and he came through the window and sadly, there was no bed to stop his fall. Once, again, Eveleth women are smarter.

Grandma Mary Boben had scarlet fever as a young teen, lost her hair (she said it was auburn and beautiful) and her hearing from it, and was pretty much deaf until hearing aids came along. She was a piece of work. She was one of the biggest sports fans I've ever met. She loved her Minnesota North Stars and sports in general. When I played football in high school, she taped all the radio broadcasts on WEVE. My favorite parts were when you could hear her cheering when we scored or moaning when we got a penalty. I still have the tape from the Virginia game and hearing her voice is my favorite part.

2. The Neighborhood

I grew up on one of Eveleth's main thoroughfares, Jones Street. Now everyone knows that the streets and avenues in Eveleth are named for presidents. I still haven't figured where "Jones" came from. Our house was at 608 Jones Street. Jones Street ran from the main drag, Grant Avenue, all the way to the eastern edge of town, an area called Morningside, I assume, because the sun appears to rise in the east. As a kid, I'd hear the motorcycles and hot rods roar by at night as there were no stop signs for the three blocks up from Grant Avenue.

Our house sat between houses owned by Frank and Mary Marasco and Primus and Rose Skumatz. Both Frank and "Prim" were World War I veterans. Prim was from St. Cloud originally and Frank and Mary immigrated from Italy when they were in their late teens. Rose was one of those old-fashioned telephone operators. The ones in front of the switchboard asking, "Number please?"

Frank had two apple trees that provided much of my fruit intake as a kid. Sometimes he was ok with me picking apples and sometimes not. I can still taste them. By the way, Frank looked just like "Chef Boyardee." He died when I was in junior high. Later, Mary would call me up and ask me to come over for pizza. This was not the kind of pizza most of us were used to. It was authentic, homemade, thick-crusted Italian pizza like only a true Italian could make. Almost like bread, really, with lots of sauce and just a bit of cheese. I loved it and stuffed my face as she told me stories about the old days, how she and Frank met, etc.

Rose and Prim were like grandparents to my sister and me. I'd help him with yard work and other chores. He'd always ended his yard work with a shot of whiskey and a beer--usually Michelob. He pronounced it "Mishelobe." Sometimes he drank Metaxa, a Greek liquor. I think I was about five years old when I started drinking a bit of beer with him. Rose always gave me 7 Up in a Styrofoam coffee cup. I'd drink that and Prim would pour beer in the cup for me to sip on.

"Don't tell Rose," He'd always say.

We'd sit in his backyard and talk. Sometimes my dad would wander over and enjoy a shot and a beer too. This always occurred around 11am which is a great time for summer drinking if you ask me.

Rose used to give me toast and honey when I visited. I remember looking out our living room window into their small kitchen window and see Prim doing dishes. I've always remembered that. If a WWI vet can do dishes, then all men should. It was easy to see that Rose ran the show in their house. Once again, another fantastic Eveleth woman.

Across the alley, off B Avenue, lived another couple who were like grandparents to me: Bridget (Biddy) and Charlie (Poosh) Perushek. Sadly, both of them died young, Biddy of cancer and Charlie of a heart attack. Both were in their early 50's if I remember that correctly. Biddy might actually have been in her late 40's. I knew their sons, Jeff and John, well and they were like brothers even though they were much older. My favorite story about them:

They had a huge set of those little army men that were so popular years ago. They were made of plastic and the set had trucks, tanks, airplanes, etc. I believe the set came with both American men in green and Germans in gray. Anyhow, they spent hours setting it all up in the backyard. They also had a brick of firecrackers and wound all the fuses together and intertwined them among all the men, tanks, trucks, and planes. They lit the main fuse and pretty much blew up their whole army setup in less than a minute. I heard the firecrackers and ran over just in time to see the backyard on fire and Poosh yelling and screaming at them as they were stomping out all the mini fires they created. Classic! Only in Eveleth. I still see Jeff on the third of July and it's always a treat to check in with him.

    Another fascination was watching Poosh make the old-time goalie masks with the plaster. I would see him do this, usually in the summer, and go over to watch. The goalie would lay flat on a long lawn chair and Poosh would apply the plaster to the contours of the goalie's face. It took several layers and the goalie would have to lay still for a few hours for it to dry. I'm pretty sure Bruce "Mokie" Orehek was one of the goalies who had this done as were other Region 7 goalies from other schools. Poosh was the go-to guy if you needed a new mask. It was pretty fun to watch and the masks were always cool. Old time hockey! (Update, 2022: I saw "Mokie" at the Red Garter on July 3, 2022, and he told me that *his* masks were made by Virginia's Doc Stanaway!)

My play in the neighborhood was limited until I learned to ride a bike. Then the town was there for exploring. Like all Eveleth kids in the 70's, we wandered around causing trouble and playing with friends until it was time for dinner. (Did you ever watch the Bad News Bears movies from the 1970's?) We never worried much about lunch and our parents were usually working anyway. Lunch for me was often apples stolen from the many trees in town. Since Eveleth was an immigrant town, many of the apple trees were grown from seeds brought over from the European countries the people originated from, mostly in the late 1800's and into to the early 1900's.

My mother later bought one of those boat horns that she would give three loud blows from when it was dinnertime or time to come home. I could hear that a mile away. I'm not kidding. When I heard those three blasts, I'd had better hightail my behind home as fast as I could. And I did. You know, Mom. She might get pissed.

I lived just a short block from the old Eveleth Junior High. The large rectangular plot of land facing Jones Street was the football field for my friends Ross Richards, Craig"Figgy" Ritacco, Chris Spragg, Scott McNulty, and Tommy Warn. We must have played hundreds of games of tackle football. Lots of bloody noses, grass-stained jeans, and bruises for sure. The side facing Adams Avenue was our baseball side. We played with a tennis ball mostly and the far end with the concrete wall and the iron railing was the home run fence. I remember Ross had the best swing and he could jack 'em on a pretty regular basis. Good times.

One of the best things to do was play our version of hide and seek. Now there was a twist to this game and at times, it was painful. We all had the best toy of the day a slingshot called a "Wrist Rocket." It was a pretty well-built slingshot with sturdy handles and a rubber hose with a leather pocket to hold whatever you wanted to shoot. Down at Craig Ritacco's neighborhood, there was a large, castle like house across the street from his place. The owners didn't seem to mind that we played there, climbed their trees and wreaked havoc whenever we had the chance. They had at least one of those crab apple trees with the small red sour apples. Those babies fit perfectly inside of the slingshot pocket and flew very nicely when shot. Our hide and seek game was more hiding than anything because if you saw a player from the enemy's team, you unloaded on him with the wrist rocket. The best was if you were lucky enough to hit someone in the back of the thigh as they were running. It would usually drop them like a bad habit. We usually left those wars with a few bruises on our arms and legs. So much fun!

    Hunting and fishing were a huge part of growing up on the Iron Range. When I did hunt with my dad, our favorite part was cruising the dirt roads of Zim and Forbes, Minnesota, in search of the elusive ruffed grouse. We walked quite a bit but also just cruised the roads, drinking pop and eating chips while listening to Ray Christianson call the Gopher football games on the radio. There were miles and miles of dirt roads in Zim and Forbes. I had a real cool single shot .410 shotgun. You had to be a decent shot to shoot anything with a .410 as the shot pattern was so small. I still have my pump .20 gauge in my mud room. I shot grouse, ducks, rabbits, pigeons, snakes, squirrels, crows, and other things with that shotgun. I haven't shot it in probably 30 years but I still have it.

    I fished quite a bit on my own. I rode my bike to the Ely Lake beach to fish off the fishing pier in the spring. I also liked the boat landing area on St. Mary's opposite the entrance to the Ely Lake Park. I usually spent time bobber fishing with night crawlers or casting spoons or spinners.

    I spent a lot of time "picking" night crawlers in my yard and neighborhood. I'd get the grass wet at dusk and wait until they'd come out of their holes and lay on the dewy grass. I could easily get several dozen in an hour's time. I kept them in the garage in a cooler with ice blocks I'd steal from my parents' fridge. My neighbor, George Yurkovich, used to come over and give me a few bucks for all the crawlers he needed for his weekly trips to the St. Louis River. I anxiously waited for him to return. He almost always had a few fish with him. Mostly northerns and the occasional walleye.

    My neighborhood friend, John Kleven, and I had a cool arrangement with this guy who had a basement minnow business. He lived directly across from Poor Gary's (Bridgeman's then) and John and I started trapping leeches for him in Fayal Pond. We never got paid but he let us pick out some lures from his collection he sold. We also brought crappies and sunfish to Oscar Kaner, at his Army Surplus Store who had let us take some lures in return. I remember exploring the back room at Oscar's and look at all the Army stuff he had for sale in his surplus store. I bought a cool green army bag with a strap I used when I hunted. Later, in high school, Mike Hallstrom and I bought these cool Army trench coats that must have been at least 40 years old at the time.

I had a lot of fun hunting and exploring the woods behind Fabiola Bluff and The Eveleth Vocational School. My partner on these trips again was John Kleven. We often spent the whole day hunting, hiking, target shooting, whatever. During the fall teachers' strike of 1981, we spent almost every day there from dawn to dusk. We used to walk there and pass our teachers walking the picket line who wished they could have gone hunting with us. There were a lot of deer back there and I don't believe many people hunted that area. I knew every square foot of those woods.

    Many years later, while staying with my wife Traci and daughters at the Super 8, we hiked up on top of Fabiola and picked blueberries. It's mostly grown over now and you can barely see the bluff from the highway.

    My favorite hunting was on the Red Lake Indian Reservation with Dick Lawrence. When his boys Tom (who is now my brother-in-law) and Bob were in college or had moved away, I became the next hunting partner for Dick. We took a few trips up to the reservation during my junior high and high school years. You could never call the time of year "deer season" or "fishing season" at the reservation as there were *no* seasons. We often packed shotguns, rifles, and fishing rods for the same trip. We were often with Dick's half-brother "Buster" who lived in Bemidji. We'd pick him up and head north to the reservation and sleep in the truck, a camper, or in a tent. I slept under a canoe once.

My favorite part was "shining" deer. We'd hunt grouse and ducks all day on the many roads up there, take an early evening nap and get up after dark, usually 10 or 11pm. We'd hook up some powerful spotlights to the truck battery and cruise the many farm fields in search of night feeding deer. The spotlight would light up their eyes a bright green or yellow. That's what you aimed at. It was all you could usually see unless you caught one up close. I was usually light guy #2. Dick or Buster were the shooters mostly and sometimes Tom when he was there.

My best memory is of Dick shooting at a deer standing in a ditch with his .44 magnum, a gun called "The Thompson Contender" from the passenger seat of the truck. I once shot a swimming duck while sitting between Dick and Buster in the truck with Buster holding the barrel of my shotgun so it wouldn't kick back up at him and spill the beer he was holding. Good times.

We also made a fun ice fishing trip in February one time and caught many walleye. I was in 8th grade, I believe, and Tom and I drank a few Hamm's beers while having to walk through very deep snow to get out to the where we would cut our holes. I was wearing an old military trench coat, long underwear, and everything else needed while ice fishing. I had a six pack of beer in each pocket of the trench coat along with one more I was holding. I was playing the human version of Tom Lawrence's pack mule. We had to walk like a mile. Red Lake is level, sandy, and not real deep. Just to get to a water level over 5 ft meant a long walk. This was ice fishing out in the open. No fancy ice houses with TV's. We slept in the truck that night. I loved that area of the state and it was one of the reasons I later attended Bemidji State University for college.

3. The Eveleth Golf Course

I still tell my third graders that golf is the greatest sport of all. It's social, you are always outdoors, and it was always fun. The worst day on the course is always better than the best day at work. (I stole that line.)

I don't really have many memories about the summer months that didn't involve golfing or working at the golf course. I think I spent 95% of the summer vacation days either working or golfing at the course from the time I was about 10 or 11 years old until I moved to the twin cities at 25.

Golf started simply for me. I'd walk around with my dad as he played the course. I was more interested in walking into the woods to find golf balls. When I did get a small set of clubs, my golfing consisted of hitting shots on the side of the public library grounds on Pierce Street. There was a small creek bed that ran at the end, right below where the Eveleth Hospital was. I remember hitting a five iron a lot. The distance was probably 60 yards at most. Later, I got the idea to put electricians' tape on some of those hard plastic golf balls with holes. I played in between my house and the neighbors' houses and learned to hit fades, hooks, and trick shots to avoid bouncing balls off windows and siding. It was a practice I continued for years, even in high school.

My first full rounds of golf started when I was around eight years old. I played mostly with my dad for the first year or so. He always laughed when I used the ball to pound the tee into the hard, dry turf with the ball like a hammer and nail.

Learning to play on the Eveleth course gave you an advantage that playing other courses could not. It was hilly, tight, and very dry, especially in late summer. You needed to be accurate and play the many bumps and irregularities of the course. Eveleth players are usually very accurate and have great short games. As my game progressed, I spent many summer days out there. I'd usually get a ride from my dad or mom and hang out in the clubhouse or on the practice green and wait for friends to show up and play. The course was never busy on weekdays and we usually played a couple of rounds most days.

The old clubhouse was a great place to hang out and the employees never seemed to mind a few kids being around. They used to have a "locker room" which was just a storage room with these big wooden lockers you could rent for the year. We all kept our clubs and shoes in the lockers and I also had swim trunks and a fishing rod as St. Mary's Lake was on the 5th hole and we often fished and swam when we got tired of golfing.

Among my friends at the course were the Tusa twins: Keith and Kevan, Andy Williams, Jim Kennedy, Pat Forte, Joe Delich, Brian Raduenz, Paul Janisch, Scott Spier, Craig "Slick" Holgate and Brad Windfeldt. Later, most of us made up the Eveleth high school golf team. Joe played on the tennis team. He should have played golf! We had so much fun, often playing for what little money we had. We made each other better players and had a lot of laughs. There's nothing like learning to play pressure golf when you are playing for your lunch money.

Since I spent so much time on the course it was inevitable that I'd start working there. I joined the crew and worked with Keith, Kevan, Andy, Jimmy, and Brad. I think I was about 13 years old when I started. Our first crew boss was Doug Tusa, the twins' older brother. He pushed us hard and the course looked better than it had before.

A big change came in 1984 when the first fairway watering system was installed. It changed the course quite a bit. Areas where little grass grew softened and saw new growth, you took divots that were dirt instead of sand, and the course inevitably played longer. Since then, a new and better system has been installed and the course is at its best now and it certainly plays much longer than it did in the old days. You get no more "August roll."

Around that time, the old clubhouse was razed and room was made for a new one. For most of one year, there was a trailer parked above the ninth green where you hung out, had your drinks, etc.

The Eveleth golf team had much success in the early 80's making a couple of trips to the state tournament. We also won our share of conference meets and invitationals. I still think it was the highlight of being in high school. You got to miss a fair amount of school to play golf! My daughter,

Lauren, played for the Champlin Park Rebels girls' team and she was the envy of a few of her friends who wished they could have had permission to skip school to play golf.

Writing about the time spent golfing in Eveleth would fill a whole book. There were many funny stories and some that are better left unsaid. One that was remembered: During our senior year, we traveled to International Falls to play an 18-hole meet. We got to miss school so that made it extra special. I don't remember the Falls Country Club having a driving range but, rather, a field in which we could hit some warm up shots. Kevan Tusa and I were hitting a few long irons in this field. He striped a two or three iron low and screaming toward the far end of the field. There was an old pickup truck parked there. His shot hit the windshield of the truck and we were close enough to see that there was a large crack in it. Needless to say, we quietly snuck away from the scene of the crime and no one saw us. A few minutes later, near the clubhouse, we hear someone yelling and screaming about his broken windshield. Evidently, it was a truck owned by one of the Falls players. Hopefully, this rattled him a bit because I remembered that we won the meet that day!

There were many fun days working outside on the crew. My favorite times were getting the course ready for the big tournaments. This involved working sometimes in the early evening to cut greens and select hole placements. For some reason, we thought different rules applied to nighttime working. I can remember slugging from a half pint of root beer schnapps as I rode along changing the cups and raking the traps. It was night after all. We were usually in the bar at that time.

At the time, chewing tobacco was popular. Most of the guys on the crew chewed while working. I could not ever develop a taste for Copenhagen, their chew of choice. I liked the minty flavor of Hawken. It was probably the weakest of the chews you could buy but I just liked the spitting part of it anyway.

In March of 1985, I had the special opportunity to travel with Steve "Tuna" Taft and my golf team teammate, Brad Windfeldt, to the home of golf,

Scotland. We played golf for nine days and played a few of the courses in the current rotation of the Open Championship: St. Andrew's, Muirfield, Royal Troon, and Royal Turnberry. It was an unforgettable trip and one that would probably be unaffordable nowadays. I loved the history and all the uniqueness of the courses over there. It's really a different game as the wind plays such a huge part. You play the ball much closer to the ground. High ball hitters would struggle over there. It was wet and cold most days but us Eveleth guys, we were used to it. For years, I said my best round ever was a 46-46--92 I shot in the cold rain at Royal Muirfield, often billed as the hardest course in the rota of the Open Championship.

    The drinking age over there was 18 so I had the chance to enjoy "legal" drinking for the first time. I drank vodka and sour then but the Scots called sour "lemonade." We had tons of fun in a few pubs and restaurants during our time there. We met two guys in the pro shop at North Berwick and they told us to stop by this wedding reception they were going to in the same hotel we were staying at. It was crazy. The bride's father gave me a cigar and we had way too many drinks. Good times.

Since so many people from the wedding were staying at the hotel also, we were each given a tiny room for ourselves that night. "Tuna" did not take part in that night's festivities with Brad and me but rather went to a pub alone. All the pubs in Scotland close at 11pm. When we left the reception, we went to his room, woke him up, and proceeded to try our best AWA Wrestling holds on him. I think Brad picked him up and body slammed him on the floor! Needless to say, Tuna did not speak to us for a full day after. That's what you get for taking two 18-year-olds to Scotland.

I remember prior to the Scotland trip, I had to get a form signed so I could get make up schoolwork or whatever I was going to miss while on the trip. I went to the Principal Melgeorge's office. I told him where I was going and how long, etc. After giving me the most disgusted look a principal ever gave me, he told me I probably couldn't find Scotland on the large world map on his office wall. I said I could and promptly pointed it out. That seemed to make him angrier and he quickly signed the form and told me to get lost. I think that was polite Mr. Melgeorge. You did not want to anger that guy. Ever.

I later spent a ton of time with Tuna in Edina. Shortly after moving to the Twin Cities to teach school, he got me a job at a small executive golf course in Edina near the Southdale Mall called Normandale. He was working at Edina's city-owned Braemar Golf Club and they ran the course I worked at. Most Saturdays all spring and summer, Tuna and Greg "Seve" Delich and I would meet at Braemar and play 18 holes in the late afternoon after Tuna and I finished our morning work shifts. These were often money games with tons of beer in the cart. I remember having a soft suitcase-like cooler that we would fill with Special Export Light. It held 20 cans. I was good for two beers each nine and Tuna would drink the remaining 16 beers. Of course, the official course rule was you could only drink beer you purchased at the course but we were employees after all and no one seemed to mind. I never made much more than minimum wage at the Edina course but I would have done it for all the free golf we played.

I remember we played at 4:00pm every Saturday all spring, summer, and fall for a few years, it was fun to come to the 8th tee at Braemar which was next to the clubhouse. Braemar did good business catering wedding receptions so there was always a wedding reception crowd watching us tee off on #8.

4. Slinging Drinks in a Drinking Town

Another one of my jobs was the morning cleaner at Eveleth's best bar: The Roosevelt. Bob Delich owned the bar from the mid 70's until it was sold about 15 years later. My first trips to the bar were on Saturday afternoons when my dad and I would stop after spending time at the sauna in Virginia. I must have been five or six years old. I remembered it being packed and smoked-filled on those afternoons and Bob was usually behind the bar. Dad would sit me on a bar stool and I'd have a cold bottle of grape or orange pop. In those days, you could get the best pop in glass bottles. Dad would have a drink and shoot the bull for a while. I was fascinated by watching Bob make drinks. I still enjoy sitting on a barstool and watching a bartender craft a nice cocktail. Especially if it is for me!

    Much later, I got the cleaning job at the bar. Joe Delich did it for years and passed it on to Paul "Ace" Coldegelli. Paul entered the Navy and the job was given to me. It was a good job to have but it meant getting up very early before school. In the summer months, I cleaned the bar before going to my job at the golf course.

    Around this time, my dad began managing the bar at the Eveleth Elks Club. Soon after, when I was 19, he trained me to begin bartending. I learned from him and his main bartender, John Curphy. John taught me a lot about making drinks, lighting cigarettes for customers, how to properly clean glassware and the bar top, etc. I learned early on to make many fancy cocktails like the Manhattan, Old Fashioned, etc.

    We had a ton of fun working the many weddings, curling bonspiels, and class reunions at the bar. I especially enjoyed working the weddings and meeting people from out of town. They always marveled at how cheap the drinks were. I think, if I remember right, a bar pour cocktail or a bottled beer at the time I started was 90 cents. This would have been late 1985. I also got to work with Guy "Guy Gadwa" Cuppoletti and Jack "Berkie" Berquist. Good times for sure.

After a couple of years at the Elks, I moved downtown to work at the Roosevelt. This was high energy pouring for sure although I loved the day shifts and asking the World War II veterans questions about their experiences. The Roosevelt is still a legendary bar and easily the best one in town.

When I moved to the Twin Cities to teach school, I was able to get a job bartending for D'Amico Catering Company at which one of the head people at the time was my classmate, Craig "Figgy" Ritacco. I spent one year pouring drinks at wealthy people's house parties and some larger events. Didn't quite make the same money there as I did on a busy night at the Roosevelt and I found most of those folks not as fun or interesting as your average Iron Ranger.

Bartending has become more of a craft now with the special ingredients, flavored liquors, and tons of locally brewed beers. These folks can surely make a great drink but can they handle a crowd six-deep at 8:30am on Fourth of July morning in Eveleth? Probably not.

5. School in Eveleth

Any Eveleth resident will tell you their main education came in the bars, boats, hunting shacks, and golf courses of the Iron Range. I think whomever invented the term "school of hard knocks" must have been an Eveleth resident. But we did attend regular school. I never was able to learn many stories from my grandparents regarding school as all of them, with the exception of my Grandma Mary Intihar, quit school in the 6th or 7th grade. Grandma Mary Boben had to due to losing her hearing from scarlet fever and my grandfathers had to go to work to support their families as many men of that era were forced to do.

I tell my third graders that I had the best education as not only were the teachers teaching us but, being in a small town, everyone was a teacher to us in some way. We just watched what the older kids did.

I caused a fair share of trouble at Franklin Elementary School considering that I had two uncles and an aunt who taught there. I couldn't sit still and focus well but I generally did well in the early grades. No one had talked about *Attention Deficit Disorder* in those days but I'm sure it affected many of us. I spent quite a bit of
time in the hallways of Franklin Elementary when the teachers got sick of me.

When I was in college training to be a teacher, we were reading an article about this newly discovered ADHD and the symptoms were listed in the article. I instantly realized that I was an ADHD sufferer and it all made sense. I had struggled with memorizing what I've read and had difficulty in college lecture courses when teaching meant they just talked at you. If I had to write a paper or do some sort of project, it was much easier than taking a test on the material. I'm a classic bullshitter so writing on any subject came easy. As a teacher now, it's easy for me to recognize these symptoms in children and they are very common now. Often, ADHD children are very bright students. They struggle with the focus to take in all the material and I always keep that in mind when teaching them.

    The highlight of my years at Franklin was having my uncle, Bobo Kochevar, as my sixth-grade teacher. He was tough on me and I gained absolutely no advantage being his nephew. He made me sit right in front of his desk all year and would not let me change my seat. I still enjoyed the year immensely and my teaching style today closely resembles Bobo's as he was tough and firm but loved his kids. You could always tell how much he cared for you and would do anything to help you be successful. I'm still learning things every day as a teacher. After 32 years of doing it, it still is a learning experience every day and every class and child is unique.

My uncle, "Demo" Mayasich, was also a teacher at Franklin. I spent time being a substitute teacher for both of them during the first year out of college. If I remember right, that year was also Demo's last year as a teacher before he retired.

I remember one time in sixth grade when my Peewee A hockey team was going to play in the state tournament in Albert Lea. Demo called me over to his room to wish me luck the day before our team left. He held out his hand to shake mine and he had palmed a $20 bill into it. That was quite a bit of cash for a kid in 1979. It's a special memory for me and one of the thousands of reasons I have such cool uncles. It just so happened that my Uncle Bill was the assistant hockey coach at Albert Lea High School at the time and he provided my team with all the extra tape we could use and the best locker room at the arena.

A former Evelethian, Roy Nystrom, was the head coach in Albert Lea and continued in that job for many years after. It must have been fun for Bill and Roy to have a bunch of Eveleth people at the arena.

I remember quite a bit about the years at Franklin School. Playing marbles at recess, king of the hill on the huge snow piles in the winter, wrestling and fighting, throwing snowballs at each other and trying not to get caught. If I remember right, fighting and throwing snowballs was an offense that earned you a paddle on the backside. The paddles, or "Boards of Education" were usually made of old goalie sticks. I seem to remember that most of the men teachers had one as they must have been the "designated paddlers" of the day. I think at least one of the teachers made you sign the board if you got whacked with it. It must have surely been a moment of pride. I don't remember getting the paddle as I must have been smart enough not to get caught throwing snowballs and fighting or just lucky as I did plenty of both. Mike Hallstrom told me that he once got the paddle for having a cool "naked lady" pen which, when you turned it upside down and the ink flowed downward, you saw some nakedness.

Attending junior high and high school was fun too. I learned by 7th grade that causing too much trouble was just going to be an inconvenience for me so I settled down quite a bit. Either that or the principal, Robert Mohn, scared the crap out of me. Probably the latter. Playing sports in school meant you had to behave in class. I was not going to give up missing school to play golf meets in the spring. Those years were a blur but I remember being in the class plays, playing golf, and playing football. Don't we all just remember those parts? Who remembers a day in class? I don't. I was very shy so just sort of blended in most of the time.

There were so many fun things happening in school. None of it had to do with being in class. The teachers were good and they left you alone, mostly, if you behaved and tried hard. My behavior was pretty good from 7th to 12th grade as I realized it was going to be very inconvenient to get detention.

6. Characters

We've all met our favorite Eveleth characters and have our favorite stories. Depending on the era in which you grew up, you had the people you met or knew. If you had a long Eveleth lineage, you knew through your parents and grandparents who the characters were and you heard the stories.

The Tusa twins were characters. Spending a ton of time in a canoe or on the golf course with them provided me with enough material to write their biographies. Aside from being great athletes, they were always into something interesting or they were fighting. As a father of twins, I see mine do so many things that remind me of Keith and Kevan. The arguing, etc. just brings back so many memories of the boys on Golf Course Road.

Keith and Kevan (yes, it's –an) had a canoe. It was pretty small, perfect for two guys fishing on St. Mary's and crowded for three. I was often the third as we paddled around trying to find schools of crappies. Sometimes it was Keith and me, or Paul Janisch, or Brad Windfeldt. We all loved fishing.

Crappies were the main target as St. Mary's Lake was loaded with them. But they were small. St. Mary's did have walleye, we found out. Kevan was bass fishing one early evening and hooked what he thought was a huge largemouth. It turned out to be an 8-pound walleye! I bet he still has the picture of himself holding it. I bet he'd put that fish in his top three catches ever! After that, we switched our gear and went after walleye for a bit. I remember catching a few on nightcrawlers but not many.

    Once, Keith and I were in the canoe fishing alongside the shore by the 4th hole. Kevan found out that Keith had taken the canoe when he wanted it and found us. After screaming at Keith from the shore to bring it in, he started throwing rocks at us. Now, this canoe was tippy when you were not moving around. Trying to fish and dodge rocks at the same time was a challenge. After a few minutes, Kevan cooled down and left. Good thing. He was so mad.

    The Tusa boys were smart businessman. They always seemed to have an ID of one of their three older brothers. This provided them to chance to buy alcohol at about 15 or 16 years old. The legal age then was 19. I once went with Keith to the Liquor Locker in Virginia where, after cashing his golf course check, he spent a couple of hundred dollars on beer and liquor. He kept a little for himself and later drove out to the high school party hangout in the woods to sell the rest at a hefty profit. In those days, a quart of Windsor was about $6. He could get $12 or more easily. A case of Hamm's or Pabst was purchased for about $6 tops but could bring in triple that. It was a nice side job for Keith. Of course, those woods' parties usually involved kegs and $2-3 was all you needed for a plastic cup with all your drink refills. Good times.

7. They Called Him "Doc."

As I write this it is a few days after the funeral of an Eveleth legend and a one-of-a-kind guy. His real name was Ray Martinson. Very few people knew him as Ray. He was a doctor so he was called "Doc." I know, very original.

Doc was like a member of our family. He spent almost every Sunday morning eating breakfast at our house. He also stopped by a couple of weeknights every week to read the paper and hang out with my parents. Over the years, he helped me with algebra, took me flying in his plane, and told countless Eveleth stories.

Doc was the team doctor for the Eveleth sports teams and if you played sports at Eveleth High School over the years, you had him give you your physical. Doc was on the sidelines or at the hockey rink for thousands of games over the years.

I still remember his unique way to fix a separated shoulder. He took off his shoe and placed his foot in the player's armpit, pulled and twisted the arm and the shoulder popped back into place. Usually, the player went back into the game.

When I was in sixth grade, I got a concussion playing hockey. I spent the early evening vomiting. Instead of a trip to the hospital, my mom just called Doc. He must have thought it was serious because he stayed in my family's rec room that night while I slept on the couch and woke me every hour as he told me later concussed patients can die if left to sleep. That's Doc. To this day, I still have not ever had a general doctor. The rare times I was ill I just went to urgent care and if they asked me my primary doctor was, I told them I didn't have one. They always gave me strange looks. When I started out as a new teacher, you'd be ill a lot with strep throat and ear infections as you'd catch stuff from the students before you built up some immunity. I hardly ever went to a doctor. I just called Doc and he asked where I wanted to pick up my prescription. He used to call whatever pharmacy I told him to and after giving his doctor's prescription code, he would tell them a story about me. I think they must have thought he was nuts. Sometimes, when I picked up my prescription, instead of my name on the label, it said, "Tommy Two Shoes."

8. Bars and More Bars (And Johnny's Warehouse)

Eveleth is known for its bars, or as my Grandfather Tony Boben called them, saloons. He should know. He spent many many hours in the bars of Aurora and Eveleth and probably other places too. My dad worked as a bartender at Perk's Corner Bar, (Now the drive-in bank)
Mr. Mitch's (now Boomtown) and Bob's Roosevelt. He also managed and tended bar at the Eveleth Elk's Club. Because of this, I also spent time in the bars visiting him when he worked the dayshift, bringing him lunch, and if I was lucky, enjoying a bottle of grape or orange pop while sitting at the bar. I was too young when he was at Perk's but I remember Mitch's and the Roosevelt quite clearly.

I learned how to play pool from Mitch's son, Pete "Zoner" Batinich at Mitch's when I was seven or eight years old. Some of the first money I earned was working for Mitch. I'd clean up the parking lot, the downstairs beer storage area, and help my dad clean the bar on Saturday mornings. Mitch was always good to me and gave me a few bucks here and there and let me drink all the Coke and eat all the chips I wanted.

To this day, I love being in bars, especially older, working-class dive bars. I don't even need to have a drink. My blood pressure goes down when I walk into an old bar.

Some summers, my dad drove a beer truck for the legendary Johnny Karakas, who owned the Hamm's distributorship down the hill from the end of the south side of Grant Avenue. I often got to go with Dad on trips to deliver beer. I was pretty good at using the two-wheeler to haul empty cases of returnable longneck bottles out to the truck while my dad hauled in the full ones. We visited Chisholm, Hibbing, Aurora, and Biwabik to deliver Hamms kegs and bottles to the establishments in those towns.

Johnny was also very good to me. I was the kid who wore the Hamm's hats and tee shirts to school as Johnny always had some for me. I also had all the stickers I wanted and a beer light in my bedroom. I had a Hamm's Bear calendar thing in my bedroom for many years. It was the Hamm's Bear holding these blue cubes where you change them to show the date. It even had little cards for the months. I later gave it to my buddy Mike Hallstrom who had a Hamm's collection.

I still remember John's wife, Eve, sitting at her desk going over invoices and working the phone taking orders. She often had a can of beer on her desk. Surprisingly, they had no running water there but there was plenty of beer to drink!

Johnny used to always ask me how old I was. He told me when I turned 16, I could come work for him. But by that time, I was a few years into my job at the golf course.

9. Coach McKenzie

The years 2016-2017 brought some notable deaths to the Eveleth community. Doc Martinson, Pat Forte, and Coach Bill McKenzie. All were well known and of great influence to other Eveleth folks in their own way.

I had the opportunity to know Coach McKenzie well as a member of the golf team in high school and as the hockey manager during my 8th and 9th grade years. He also coached the 10th grade football team and was one of the phy ed. teachers for Eveleth schools. Coach was really funny at times. The hockey teams during the early 80's did not have the same success as the iconic teams of the 40's through the 70's. They were decent, but not quite deep playoff teams like earlier years. Because of this, I had a front row seat to some of Coach's best lines as he had to berate his teams during the locker room intermissions. I'm sure everyone who played for him had their favorite lines. He often described a slow skater as "having a refrigerator on their back." He hated when a player raced around the rink but didn't accomplish much or get in on the action.

    Coach was great as our golf coach too. He would play a few holes with us when we played daily in Eveleth during the season. His short game was awesome and he had good feel on and around the greens which is usually the case with hockey players. I don't think Coach ever hit a drive longer than maybe 225 yards but I saw him shoot 36 or 37 a few times when he was into his 50's.

One time we were in the golf team station wagon and were racing up to Ely to play a nine-hole meet. I think Coach was in a hurry because somewhere south of Ely, we came around a corner and a highway patrol was stopped in the opposite lane with his lights on. Coach took this as a signal to stop. He rolled down the window and the highway patrol just said, "Slow down." There were a few snickers in the golf car after that one. I'm pretty sure that meet was the one we played where it began snowing halfway through the round and played the last four holes with an inch of powder on the course and more coming down. My hands were so cold and wet that I played the last three holes with just my 7 iron so I didn't have to take the time to switch clubs. I even putted with it.

Another favorite Coach McKenzie memory is of him being the main gym teacher I had throughout elementary school. We had our gym classes in that large rectangular room on the end of the second (or third) floor at the Franklin School. It also was used for the music classes if I remember right.

My favorite activity throughout my years of gym class was floor hockey. When we had the games in the music/PE room, it got pretty crowded so we'd play in shifts. When you were not playing, you sat on the edge of the little stage at the far end and watched and waited. When I got the puck, I often would not think of scoring a goal, but rather, try to make my best wrist shot and hit any of the people who were watching from the stage. The best was when you got someone in the forehead when they were not paying attention. Now Coach knew what us hockey players were up to and usually a warning if you did it once would suffice but sometimes you got away with it more than once. I remember getting someone right in the chin with the puck and looking over at Coach and seeing him trying to stifle a smile as I must have hit someone he didn't like! Great memory.

When I was in 10th grade, I took PE as an elective. Most of my good friends did also. Coach was the teacher but he mostly just let us play whatever we wanted every day and he watched a bit then hung out in Coach Lawrence's office. Of course, floor hockey was the choice most days but these games did not much resemble the games in elementary school. We had the full main gym (or half of it) and these games were total chaos: slashing, fighting, pushing, crosschecking, hacking, swearing, bloody noses, bruises, broken sticks, etc. Of course, we loved every minute of it. Some of the guys in the class who didn't want to play would sit in the stands and throw dice for money. Only in Eveleth!

10. Eveleth Sports: The 1970's

If you are an Eveleth native of a certain age, you remember the glory years of sports at the high school. I'm way too young to remember the great hockey years of the 40's and 50's although I certainly knew many of the players.

The time I remember best was the 1970's. Eveleth won the high school football championship in 1973. I was only seven years old but I can still remember the excitement of that day they won the final in Wilmar. I've heard the stories in great detail from some of the players involved and certainly while hunting with Coach Dick Lawrence and my brother-in-law Tom. My old neighbor, Jeff Perushek, remembers that championship game like it was yesterday. He once recently gave me a play-by-play review of the game. I also remember my folks going up to the high school auditorium for the celebration after the team returned with the trophy. I remember my grandmother Mary Boben babysitting my sister and me while this was going on and how much we wanted to go.

While we always remember the John Mayasich years in Eveleth hockey history, it should be remembered that the mid 70's was also a great time in Eveleth hockey history. There were many more teams playing hockey in the mid 70's than earlier and it seemed that all the section 7 teams were good, especially Grand Rapids with Eveleth-native Gus Hendrickson as coach. Hibbing, International Falls, and Greenway of Coleraine were also very good. Section 7 was always the best hockey playing section in the state in those days.

My dad had retired from refereeing high school hockey and began work as the goal judge on the lobby end of the rink. Through several seasons, I sat next to him to see those great teams in action. It was great to have Eveleth scoring on that end for two periods of each game. I can still remember how fast those guys skated in those years when the game was less physical and tight. Mark Pavelich, Craig Homala, and Dave Delich, were the ones lighting the red light the most often. All of my hockey-playing friends idolized those guys. It was very common to see several members of each graduating class going on to play in the old WCHA.

The 70's teams never made it to the state tournament, mostly because the Section 7 playoffs were so competitive. I still remember the 1976 Region final in Hibbing watching the Grand Rapids Indians beat the Golden Bears. I was with my cousin Bucko and Figgy Ritacco. We were crushed when they lost. There might have even been tears.

I remember the annual pickup game played at the Franklin rink on Christmas Eve afternoon when the college guys would return home and play with us young guys in a pickup game. My brother-in-law Tom Lawrence reminded me that they used to put a keg of beer in the snow bank for when they needed a drink and a break. Good times.

Later, when Mark Pavelich was at UMD playing for Gus Hendrickson, my mom and dad would take me to games to watch. During the Gus Hendrickson, and later, Mike Sertich years, my dad would take phone orders for tickets to the UMD games so we got free tickets and used to go to all of the Friday home games for several years. I always got to go to the locker room area at intermission and say hi to Pav and Virginia's Keith Hendrickson. I was always begging for sticks and pucks too. We also got to see Dave Delich when he was in town playing for Colorado College. One of the best things was the old Duluth arena, which was shaped like a bowl with very steep sides. If you were in the upper rows, you looked almost straight down to the ice. The stairs were steep too. I still follow UMD hockey in the newspaper and consider them my favorite college hockey team.

11. Born in Eveleth

I was born on July 31, 1966. My dad likes to tell the story of my and my sister's births often. Of course, in those days, the father was never allowed in the birthing room and the mother was left to suffer alone with the hospital staff. My dad always put it simply, "One cigarette while waiting for you, two for your sister."

I think when my sister was born in 1968, he had worked the Corner Bar that evening and came home buzzed up and was awoken by my mom a couple of hours later to go to the hospital.

At the time I was born, my parents were living in Virginia in a room rented to them at the home of Dr. George Ewens, the longtime dermatologist at the old East Range Clinic and my mom's boss for many years. I believe they had a bedroom there as those were tight times, I'm sure, for a new teacher and an LPN. My mom did not want me born in Virginia, bless her heart, and made my dad drive her to the Eveleth Hospital, which was still delivering babies in

1966. Funny thing is my mom worked at the East Range Clinic and knew everyone at the Virginia Hospital too! When my sister arrived in 1968, they lived in Eveleth and drove to Virginia for the birth as it was their only choice. I'm sure they were not happy about this. I think I teased my sister about this for years as she was the only one in the family not born in Eveleth. I'm grateful to say I was "born and raised" in Eveleth.

12. Target Practice

When my cousin, Buck Kochevar, and I were in our early teens, we started small game hunting with our dads. Like any Eveleth kid, we hunted grouse and rabbits during the small game season. Often, we had more fun just shooting our shotguns and rifles. When Buck was able to drive (a year before me) we used to hunt often at his Dad's cousin's farm south of Eveleth or the back roads of Forbes or Zim. Road hunting was often the method used in those days. We just rode around, listening to the radio and trying to find grouse or if we felt like it, we walked some of our favorite trails and old logging roads.

When we wanted to just shoot our guns, we used to go back behind Mitch's Bar (Now Boomtown) on highway 53 and find all the empty liquor bottles in his garbage and take them across the highway into the woods behind the Eveleth Vocational School and line them up and blast them with our shotguns or .22 rifles. That was always fun.

I remember one time we found a life size plywood cutout of a person back there in the woods. It must have been used as a target although that seemed kind of weird. Anyway, we must have used a few boxes of .22 shells blasting holes in that thing until it was splintering and falling apart. The people at the "Votec" must have thought WW3 was starting back in those woods.

13. Learning to Drive: Eveleth-style

I started working on the golf course when I was 13 years old so the first "vehicle" I learned to drive was one of the work carts which was an old golf cart. We also had a four-wheeler that was fun to drive, and at one point, the old Army jeep that GG Sabetti always drove around town when he was the rec director. So, I learned to drive before I was 16 years old.

The older guys on the crew even taught us young guys how to drive the big tractor that pulled the gang mowers that mowed the fairways. That was cool as it was a three-speed (I think) and you needed to learn how to work the clutch which was hard to reach when you were just 14 or 15. We used to pile the whole crew on this thing. Someone (usually one of the little guys like Jim Kennedy or myself) sat on the hood and held on to the gas cap as we went along bouncing along the fairways like you were riding a horse in a rodeo. We had a cool trailer which was built from an old pickup's bed in which we hauled trees and other debris from the course.

I once fell off that trailer and landed on my backside which really hurt for a few weeks. Many years later when I went to a chiropractor to address my back pain, he said my pelvis was turned and off center. He thought I had been in a car accident. I couldn't figure out why it was like that until I remembered falling off that trailer some 30 years earlier.

    The way I learned to drive a regular car was hunting with my dad in Forbes. I was probably 13 or 14 when I started driving the back roads near my cousin Susie Mayasich's and then husband Kevin's land. Later when I got comfortable, I drove all the time when I hunted with my dad. Often, he napped in the front seat as I drove around. That was fun. Thankfully I never got pulled over. When I turned 16 and started putting in the behind-the-wheel hours, I did them in the winter with Dick Lawrence as I had the golf course job and couldn't really do them in the summer like most kids did. My behind-the-wheel usually consisted of Dick and I doing his errands in Virginia on a Sunday afternoon or riding around in the country looking for places to hunt. Only in Eveleth!

14. "U-Da" Salentich

One of the characters in the old Eveleth days was George "U-da" Salentich. He was quite a guy. Since my dad was a bartender downtown, he got to know George quite well and I remember him coming to my house for breakfast on Saturday mornings. He drank quite a lot and usually was hung over at breakfast and chain smoking in our kitchen while my mom made him breakfast. There's a legendary story about him: His mother once asked young George to go uptown to buy some bread and eggs. On the way, he dropped into the Navy recruiter's office and joined up. Many months (or years) later he came home and his mom asked him, "Where are the eggs?" I think he must have told me that one.

My sister loved George and used to sit on his lap when she was just three or four years old. When I moved to the Twin Cities, former Evelethian Steve Cannon was still doing his afternoon show on WCCO radio and used to tell stories about George. I think George passed away when he was just short of 60 years old. Too much drink, I suppose.

George was also, as the legend goes, a train hopper or hobo. He used to say, "Coast to coast on a piece of toast." Evidently, he didn't eat much. He also coined one of my favorite sayings: You'd ask him, "Hey George, are you hungry?" His reply, "No thanks, I ate yesterday!"

It was much later when I realized why he was at our house for Saturday breakfast so often. My parents felt bad for him and that breakfast might have been one of the only good meals he had all week.

15. Mitch's Nightclub

Mitch Batanich opened his nightclub, Mr. Mitch's, in the early 1970's. My dad was one of his first bartenders. Mitch's was unlike any other bar in the area. It was much bigger and had live music a few nights a week. Now this was not music made from local bands but rather touring bands who came through the area providing loud dance music for great crowds during those years. My dad used to say the Parrish Brothers were the best and came through quite often. I'd love to know who the other bands were as I assume some were later well-known bands.

My sister and I used to go with my dad to clean the place on Saturday mornings. We would have to get on the floor and pick up the drink straws as they did not get sucked up in the vacuum very well. We often found coins or dollar bills on the floor, and the occasional purse or wallet. We'd then have to look at the driver's license to find out whose it was and make a phone call. My dad would let us put some change into the jukebox and crank the tunes while we worked. We also got to drink pop out of the mix gun and eat chips too. Even at a young age, I loved bars and being behind a bar.

I was always fascinated by the band's equipment and looked closely at the guitars and drum sets on the elevated stage. Every once in a while, a band member would be in the bar messing with the equipment or fixing something and they would always say hi and answer my questions.

The 70's was a great time for the local mines and Mitch's did great business during those years. My dad first got hearing aids in his 50's and blamed the fact that he worked the waitress pit near the stage at Mitch's and lost his hearing because of it.

Later on, the bar was bought by Carver Richards and run by Nonny Horoshak. I was one of the bartenders hired and worked one spring and summer before moving to the Twin Cities. More to come on that story.

Mitch later moved to the Twin Cities and briefly owned a bar called Mitch's All-American Tavern in downtown Hopkins. I lived in Hopkins for one year and used to go visit him at his place and play pull tabs and this cool spinning wheel they had. He was always happy to see me and would tell customers at the bar that I worked for him when I was just a little kid.

16. Red Lake Hunting (Chippewa-style)

Everyone who has ever hunted with Dick Lawrence probably has a few Red Lake stories. Dick was born and raised in Red Lake. I'm talking the town, of course. The reservation. The "Rezy." No man's land. My Uncle Bobo had a few stories and of course, Tom and Bob Lawrence have many. I also have a couple but one from my very first trip to the reservation in 1980 was the most memorable. It was where I shot my first grouse and my first duck. It's where I "shined" deer for the first time. Those trips to Red Lake were fun and the hunting (or fishing) was always great. We sometimes did both on the same day!

Dick was a legend on the reservation but one late Saturday afternoon in August, 1980, proved just how much.

I was on my first trip up there and it was just Dick and me. His half-brother Buster usually came but couldn't make this trip. We were cruising down the highway as the sun was low in the sky and directly over the horizon of the highway straight ahead.

Suddenly and weirdly, the sun seemed to be blocked for a couple of seconds. I thought nothing of it but Dick hammered the gas pedal and we took off. I had no idea what had happened. We sped about a half mile and Dick slowed down and looked into a field on his left. We could just see the wide back side of a cow moose as she ambled into a grove of trees about 100 yards into the field. It was the moose that had blocked the sun as it appeared to set over the highway.

Now, on the way to the reservation, Dick told me the one lesson I needed to know. My white Slovenian skin would not help me look like an Indian and he knew that. If, by chance, I would have gotten lost or ran into a reservation member, I was to say that I was Dick Lawrence's son. That would have evidently saved me from trouble or being run off the reservation.

Dick explained that he was going in after the moose and I should wait at the truck. He donned his waders to get through the water in the ditch and off he went with his rifle. I was expecting to hear a shot or two any minute and waited anxiously.

A few minutes later, a rusty Trans Am sped by going way over the speed limit. As it went past me and the truck, it slowed and pulled over. Oh, no. I'm in trouble now, I thought.

A Native American guy in his mid 20's wearing (I'm not kidding) a powder blue tuxedo got out of the car and asked what I was doing.

"Waiting for my dad," I replied, proud that I remembered what to say.

"Where is he?" the man asked.

"In that grove," I said, excitedly, pointing to the field. "We saw a moose!"

"No shit." He replied.

He turned around, opened his trunk, grabbed his own waders and his deer rifle. His companion, a woman about his age, starts berating him about the wedding they have to go to and how they'll be late, he'll have no time, etc.

In a matter of minutes, the powder blue tuxedo guy had traversed the creek and was on his way into the grove after the moose too!

I had two thoughts: One: Dick's going to shoot him if he's not careful, or two: Dick's going to be pissed at me for saying anything about the moose. I was really hoping I'd hear a rifle shot soon, but still, nothing.

The woman pulled out a pack of cigarettes, lit one, and sat on the hood of the Trans Am swearing to herself while I leaned on the side of Dick's truck thinking there was no way Dick wasn't going to be *really* pissed at me. And this was just a few hours into our trip!

After what seemed like an hour but was only a few minutes, the young guy comes out of the grove walking at a brisk pace. As he got closer, I saw his gaze fixed on me. He also had the look like he just came out of the principal's office and that I was to blame. As he climbed up the bank to the highway, he turned to me and said, angrily, "Why didn't you tell me your dad was Dick Lawrence!?"

He tossed his gun in his trunk, and ignoring his bitching companion, sped off to attend the wedding.

A few minutes later, Dick came out of the grove, walked up the bank and asked, "Didn't I tell you to tell people you were with me?" He laughed so I knew he wasn't angry but he was disappointed as he never did see that moose.

17. We Wanted to Be Like Evel Knievel

If you ever watched *Wide World of Sports* in the 1970's, you occasionally saw Robert "Evel" Knievel use his cycle to jump over everything from junk cars, to buses, Las Vegas fountains, and river canyons. It was really cool to watch and impressionable to young boys. Of course, we had to try it.

In those days, there were no bike helmets. You couldn't buy one if you wanted to. We just didn't wear them.

The boys in the neighborhood were Brian Hill, John Kleven, Doug Paglarini, and occasionally a Bradt boy or two. Mark "Mega" Majesich would also be around at times. The toughest part was constructing a ramp. I seem to remember Doug's dad or older brother using a couple of spare 2x4's and plywood to make us one that couldn't have been more than two feet high but it seemed, in memory, to be much taller.

We started by just racing to the ramp and going off of it. When that worked well and we built confidence, we started adding obstacles to jump. There were garbage cans, bikes laid down on the pavement, and sometimes, each other. It was fun. If you got some speed going down the alley, you could get some height and soar several yards. The landing was always a challenge as those 1970's Schwins and Huffys did not have motorcycle-quality shocks and we were often thrown off the bike on the landing and had to nurse a skinned elbow and knee. Of course, if you showed the slightest bit of discomfort, pain, or tears, you were teased mercilessly. So, you tried not to. I mean, this was Eveleth, after all. You <u>never</u> cried in front of your friends.

I don't remember any major injuries but I think someone might have lost their handlebars in midflight. That made for an interesting landing. Of course, it being Eveleth, no one ever told us not to do it. I seem to remember Don Hill, Brian's dad, even watching us do it and complimenting us on our technique. Only in Eveleth.

18. History and Patriotism: Eveleth-style

I love history. I love reading about it and watching documentaries on Netflix. I consider myself very lucky to have learned about 20th century history from many Evelethians, both family and others. If I wasn't a third-grade teacher, a college history professor would be my second choice. Or a pro golfer, but neither panned out.

My neighbors on Jones Street, as mentioned earlier, were World War I veterans. Prim Skumatz, told me many stories about the battles he was in. He always said, "Five major battles, not a scratch." I remember him talking about the Battle of the Argonne Forest which lasted 47 days and only ended with the armistice which ended the war on November 11, 1918. He told me that the battle was fought in a tree-filled forest and the men on both sides were hiding behind trees as they peeked around them to see the enemy. Prim was only about 20 years old at the time.

My biggest history lessons came working the day shift at the Roosevelt in 1989 and 1990. Pouring whiskey and brandy shots and beers to the many World War II vets who came in was educational. Being very interested, I learned through reading what questions to ask. Specific questions that showed them I had done my research. Frank "Tabor" Laurich came aground at Normandy a few days after D Day. I think he had a metal plate in his head from a war injury. "Airplane Jack" Kellett was interesting and very smart. He spent the war in England loading bombs on the bomber planes and knew the pilots well. He told of how sad he was when the pilots went on sorties and never returned.

When working at the Elks Club, I got to know Jim Stanaway a bit. He spent time in England too and met his wife there. She was a very attractive lady who was always so nice to me at the bar. I loved her accent.

Bob Bratulich was another vet with great stories. He was in Vietnam. I used to ask him questions at the Elks when I tended bar there.

The very best lessons I received were from my Great Uncle Colonel Jim Tapp. I had heard many stories about him from my folks and never met him until he came up for the 4th of July just a couple of years before he died. He lived in the state of Virginia and later, Colorado. He was around 90 when I met him. He was an ace pilot which means he shot down at least five enemy aircraft. I think he had eight confirmed kills. He flew missions in the Pacific against the Japanese. My dad said he was the first ace over Japan.

Uncle Jim and I and my dad sat at a table in the Super 8 pool room while my daughters swam and talked for about three or four hours. He told me his whole story about learning to fly in Eveleth and going into the service, etc. Amazing stories from an amazing man. The story I remember most: As the war with Japan neared the end and just before the atomic bombs were dropped in August, 1945, the plan was for a major invasion of Japan in the fall or early in 1946. Before this was to happen, fighter planes were to relentlessly bomb Tokyo and other major cities. The planes took off from a runway built on some captured island, not sure which one. Jim told me that the island was pretty far away from mainland Japan and the bomber planes could only hold so much gas and the pilots knew that they would not be able to have enough fuel to get to their target, drop their bombs, *and* fly back to their island. Some ended up landing in China. Evidently, getting an aircraft carrier closer to mainland Japan was too dangerous. The pilots were not really sure if that meant they would end up crash landing in the ocean when the fuel ran out but were still very willing to go. Luckily, when the atomic bombs were dropped, Japan surrendered and a major D Day-type invasion wasn't needed.

    Like I said, the vets were very willing to talk if they knew you had done your reading and knew specific things. They were never boastful and I'm sure, wanted to forget much of what they saw. I was very lucky they shared that information with me. At the time, most knew I was in college studying to be a teacher so maybe they wanted me to know this stuff. I still talk about these brave men to my third graders even if it isn't part of any third-grade curriculum. It's good for Americans to know how these sacrifices were made for us.

19. Hall of Fame Hockey Game: Fall, 1979 (Who are these guys?)

Years ago, the first big event of the hockey season occurred in October. The new ice was in at the Hippodrome and it was time for the annual "Hall of Fame Game." Fitting as it was, the game was in Eveleth, the real home of hockey and the US Hockey Hall of Fame.

In October 1979, Eveleth hockey fans got to see a game between my favorite college team, the UMD Bulldogs, and a bunch of college guys playing on Team USA, the team that was going to represent our country at the upcoming Olympic Games in Lake Placid, New York.

In those days, the Olympic Committee in Colorado Springs picked their team after summer tryouts and the team played together for a few months against college teams and other Olympic teams for before the Olympic tournament in February.

The Olympic roster included many college players from around the country, many of whom most local hockey fans had never heard of. Of course, the Eveleth fans had our own Mark Pavelich and Virginia fans came over to see John Harrington, the only two local players on that year's Olympic team. I assume Grand Rapids fans came over to watch Bill Baker and of course, The "Babbit Rabbit" Buzz Schneider was on the team too. So, there were a few Rangers on the team.

The game pitted the Olympic team against the UMD Bulldogs, who were missing their two best players, Harrington and Pavelich. The Hipp was packed to the roof that night. I happened to be lucky enough to watch the game from the penalty box as I sat with Archie Rauzi and Bernie Newman, the two who ran the clock and kept order in the box for many years of Eveleth High School games. I think I might have been keeping the stat book that night too.

I seem to remember the Olympic team winning the game but not by much, maybe 3-0? It was a surprise as the Olympic team was basically a college all-star team. You would have expected them to easily handle a UMD team missing their two best players. I think it took them a few months to play well and, of course, we know the end to that story.

  The one thing I do remember about that night is that the lights went out and the game had to be delayed for a while the Hippodrome crew figured out what was wrong. I remember Keith Hendrickson, the Virginia native playing for Uncle Gus Hendrickson at UMD, coming over to the penalty box and chatted with us for a few minutes as we waited for the lights to come back on. What a memory! Many Evelethians can actually say they saw the 1980 gold medal-winning team play live a few months before watching them on TV from Lake Placid.

20. I Recognize That Piano Playing

I learned to play guitar from my childhood friend Jimmy Kennedy while we lived together in college at Bemidji State. Jimmy was one of the best musicians I've ever seen and still plays and gigs in the Twin Cities as part of a couple of bands while he holds down a regular job and fathers two children.

I used to go watch Jimmy and my class of 1985 classmates Rich Mattson and Russ Bergum play when I first moved to the Twin Cities in 1992. They had a band called the Glenrustles and they were pretty big time on the local Minneapolis scene. Of course, I grew up watching them play in their high school band, The Imports.

If you ever spent time with a good piano player, you might notice that when they warm up their fingers, they often play the same parts of songs or runs on the keys. I must have heard Jimmy play the same stuff a hundred times. Plus his style was very unique in a Floyd Cramer way. He was just magic on the piano. He taught himself guitar using his dad's old electric too. What a talent.

As the years passed and I became busy with my daughters, I lost track of Jimmy and had very little time to see any of the gigs he was playing. I didn't even have a phone number for him so we lost touch for several years.

   That ended once around the year 2000. I went to the Schmidt Music store in Brooklyn Center to get a few guitar picks. I liked going there occasionally to take a break from my kids and look at and play some of the guitars they had there. This Schmidt Music was more than a store. It housed a few dozen pianos and many more guitars in their showroom plus was a distribution center somewhat with a huge storage area with pianos that were trucked out to buyers all over the Twin Cities.

   When you entered the main entrance, there was a long hallway which passed their instrument repair shop and led to the piano showroom. As I walked the hallway, I heard it. That familiar sound. The warm up, those runs, those chords, those snippets of songs. I knew that sound and I knew that familiar warm up. As I turned the corner into the large showroom, there he was. My Eveleth pal Jimmy

Kennedy working the keys on a new piano, a baby grand I think it was. He was with his wife and they were looking to purchase a nice new piano for his home. We chatted for a while and it was a thrill to see him work the keys again. What a memory.

21. The Save (and an assist from Dad)

    As I've gotten older and become a parent, there are things I understand much better now, parenting things. Sometimes, you do things to prevent conflict or just to make your life easier.

    I tell this story often to friends and it's a special (and funny) memory: I can't say that I was ever a big drinker in high school but I did find time to have a few drinks here and there. I think, #1, I was terrified of getting caught from my parents, and #2, I didn't want to get kicked off the sports teams I played on in high school. My drinking as a 16-year-old consisted of drinking a quart bottle of beer or splitting a six pack with my golf buddy Andy "Anjj" Williams. We usually found a place to tip a couple in his pickup in Virginia before we cruised the main street and looked for girls. Having a couple in you made it easier to talk to them in case we were lucky enough to find some that would talk to us.

Anyway, I did just this one early spring Friday night. I must have had more than a couple. I came home and fell asleep. Now, I tend to be a mouth breather, especially when I have been drinking. Sometime early the next morning, I was awoken by my dad as he leaned over me and cranked out the window that was behind the headboard of the bed.

"Dad, what are you doing? I asked.

"Jesus Christ, this room smells like a brewery," he replied. "Open this Goddamn window when you get home. if your mother smells this room, she's gonna be pissed off all weekend and I'm not in the mood for that." He threw in a couple more "Jesus Christs" and he was out the door.

You gotta admire Dad's attitude on this. He was making the situation work for himself. He was about 44 or so at the time and he knew how to make things easier for himself. He probably didn't give a rip that I was out drinking. He wanted a stress-free weekend with a wife that wasn't pissed off. He also, I'm assuming, was saving me from getting into big trouble. My mom, at the time, was not a big fan of drinking, having her father, my grandfather Tony, have his issues with alcohol during her growing up years. I mentioned earlier that I was terrified to get trouble and piss off my mom. She has since relaxed quite a bit and enjoys her wine with my wife Traci when she visits me and my family.

22. Walking, Walking Everywhere

So many things remind me of Eveleth, even today. When I walk my dog, Howie, in the winter and it's cold, the squeaky sound my feet make on the snow reminds me of those cold winters growing up. It seemed the winters lasted seven or eight months. Living on Jones Street, I seemed to be in the middle of everywhere I had to be like downtown, school, friends' houses, etc. so I walked or rode my bike everywhere.

Today, walking to my mailbox in the winter seems tedious and cold but I literally walked everywhere during the winters in Eveleth. Like most Eveleth kids back then, our parents worked all the time and were never home. The last thing they would have wanted to do was bring me anywhere by car.

I walked to school every day from kindergarten to 12th grade. Every day! Even when it was a -40 windchill, I walked. I never seemed to want to wear a warm enough jacket or a hat and gloves but it never seemed to bother me. I can still remember the feeling of walking into the warm school building after walking there in the January cold. It seems all Eveleth kids had a permanent runny nose for at least half a year. We were tough for sure.

I can remember being in high school and on some frigid mornings, my mom made ginger snap cookies before she left for work. I stuffed my jacket pockets with the still warm cookies and used them as a handwarmer while walking to school. Then I'd be sneaky and eat them all in study hall while being watched in the library by Marge Miller. Never got caught!

I never had my own car until my third year in college. Starting golf course work at 13 and saving money for years certainly afforded me the opportunity to buy my own used car by the time I was 17 or 18 but the folks always vetoed that. I think my dating life would have been much better had I had my own wheels then but whatever. I still had my legs and they worked well.

My friends the Tusa twins had a car and I caught rides places with them or others. They had a car we called "the red car." I can't remember the make, it might have been a Pontiac but I do remember being in it quite a bit during those high school years cruising Virginia's main drag or going to parties and games, etc. Good times.

23. Eveleth Weddings and Jeana's Catering

All Evelethians have attended Eveleth wedding receptions. Probably a few dozen when you think of it. They were mostly held at the now torn down Holiday Inn ballroom or the Eveleth Elks Club. I have attended many receptions as a guest or worked them as a bartender. The thing about Eveleth is that, being a small town, you usually saw a lot of the same people at these weddings so they had kind of a sort of "Groundhog Day" feel to them (if you have seen the movie.)

The very best thing about these receptions was the food of Eveleth's own Jeana Peterson. (I seem to remember that's how she spelled her name and I apologize to JoAnn Johnson if I got it wrong.)

The food was always the same, and it was so good. I'm guessing the out-of-town guests might have thought it weird to have pasta and red sauce on a plate with chunks of polish sausage, salad, and other range delicacies such as potica and pasties. Also, her signature broasted fried chicken. But it was loved by all and being that Jeana was the only caterer in town, it was most people's choice if you wanted to please your wedding guests.

One of her helpers during those years was Barbara Turk. During those bartending years, I was dating Barb's youngest daughter, Cheryl, so Barb or Jeana always brought me a plate of food when I was behind the bar at the Elks Club. Sometimes I'd just go back to the kitchen and eat with Jeana, Barb, and the crew. At the Elks, it was customary to close the bar while the dinner was being served in the banquet room so I always found time to eat too.

As mentioned earlier, I loved bartending at the weddings in town. The tips were great and meeting people visiting Eveleth was fun.

24. Woodworking in 7th Grade

As a new junior high school student, you had to take some of the required classes for a quarter such as home economics, woodworking, etc. These classes were fun and you learned what you were good at and what you were not so good at very quickly.

The woodworking class was with Mr. Kriska. I liked learning how to use the new machines like the electric sander and the band saw. I always loved the smell of the woodworking room and the sawdust on the floor. I don't remember us ever having much of any directions as to what we were supposed to make. I think I made a candle holder once and tried for most of the quarter to make a pair of wooden-framed glasses but never was too successful. At least I learned the engineering process (as is taught to my third-grade students) and maybe a bit of patience.

Like many teachers, Mr. Kriska, Mr. Beste, and Mr. Debevec (Mr. D) were pieces of work and always made the industrial arts classes fun. I'm sure they realized who had the talent right away and who should stay away from the dangerous machinery. One of the tricks they used to do is tell a student to go see another teacher and get "the board stretcher." I got suckered into that once by Mr. Kriska. He sent me to Beste's room to get the fictional board stretcher. I think Beste said he didn't have it and to try Mr. D. Anyway, it must have been a lot of fun to be teaching in that building.

Later in high school, I took a mechanical drawing class as an elective from Mr. Beste. There were only about 12 guys in the class and we were all friends. The drawings we made were hard but I remember I learned a lot about how to measure to $1/16^{th}$ effectively, use the T-square, etc. I remember Mr. Beste would sometimes fall asleep. We used to just let him nap while we worked on our drawings.

One of my favorite memories of high school was during the 1985 state hockey tournament. I used to attend the tourney with my dad for years before but, as mentioned earlier, I was going to take that golf trip to Scotland the week after the 1985 tournament so getting some extra days off from school wasn't going to work for my folks so I showed up to some classes on that Thursday and Friday being one of only a few kids who were not in St. Paul partying and watching hockey. When I arrived at Beste's class, I was one of two students who were there. Beste thought it would be better to just hang with him in the lounge of the industrial arts building where he bought us each a Pepsi and we watched TV for an hour. Great memory.

25. Teenage Shenanigans: Old School

One of the cool things about being a son of Eveleth natives and graduates is many of the old stories I've heard from Mom and Dad. Of course, Dad was, like many Eveleth boys and men, more likely to cause trouble and have the better stories. A favorite of mine: When Dad was in high school, they had a fun activity they used to do in the summer and fall. The old garbage dump used to be located right off highway 53 behind the furniture store across the highway from Lundgren Motors.

   Like any garbage dump, it attracted critters of all kinds who feasted on the garbage, rotting food, etc. I would assume raccoons, rats, and other nocturnal creatures would come for their nightly feast. The guys would bring their .22 rifles and a few six packs, I assume, and line up a couple of vehicles with their headlights pointing toward the garbage pile. They'd wait to see what they could shoot at and unload a barrage toward any moving target. I visualize a Civil War battlefield with the guys lined up and firing at will.

   It must have been a lot of fun to be buzzed up with your buddies blasting any unsuspecting garbage eater that was unlucky enough to get in the way. I remember him saying that once someone returned to the dump the next day to find a dead black bear who somehow must have been nearby and not seen by the shooters. I always love that story. Not for the poor bear but the fact that they were able to be left alone for some fun teenage high jinx and never had to worry about the cops, noise, or whatever.

It makes me think of my bartending days when the old guys would talk about the Eveleth cops and how they used to pull over drunk drivers and just give them rides home instead of arresting them. The good 'ol days for sure.

I always loved going to the dump with my dad or my Grandfather Tony. It had everything a young boy would like: smelly, rotten trash, hungry seagulls yapping, steam from garbage piles decomposing, and many cool things to find and maybe keep. It was like the scene in *Apocalypse Now* in which Robert Duval says, "I love the smell of napalm in the morning."

26. *Everyone* Had an Outside Drinking Spot

Talk to any Evelethian about their secret (or not so secret) high school drinking spot and they will probably remember it clearly and have a bunch of stories about it. For my era, it was what we called *Horseshoe* which was a sandpit-type area near

Horseshoe Lake, not far from the Sparta area, if I remember right. In those days, two or three bucks would get you a plastic cup and all the beer available from the kegs purchased by someone lucky enough with a fake ID or an older friend who helped them make a purchase. Great times and cheap for any high school kid. I've been to a few of those parties. Another great place was the old drive-in theater off the highway where the Lutheran church is now located. You could drive in with friends or just walk through the woods to meet friends and save your movie ticket money.

 My neighbor, Scott Bradt, worked the ticket booth at the drive-in entrance, I remember, and would usually not charge me if he saw me. I can remember the Tusa twins dropping me and a couple others on the highway and we'd run up the steep bank from the highway and just walk in. No one watched or cared.

 I also remember a spot in Gilbert off the highway on the way to Biwabik. It was behind the old Knotty Pine Liquor store where Keith Tusa would make some of his liquor purchases with me along to help carry his haul.

One time, Keith, Tommy Hilfers, myself, and one or two others were having a couple of beers back in this area between Gilbert and Biwabik that had an old road into it and was an area of rolling hills and sand piles. I was having my first beer sitting on the hood of Keith's "red car" and luckily was just able to see for a brief moment, the "cherries" on top of a Gilbert cop car as it drove in. I couldn't see any other part of the car due to the hills and long grass. "Cops!" I yelled, and instinctively, we tossed the beers, jumped into the car and sped out on the road toward the highway using the "out" road as the cops drove in on the "in" road. I don't believe the cop ever saw us as we got to the highway and sped away quickly. That was a close call.

The only time I remember getting caught was in the north side of Virginia, MN. A few of us were in a car having a few behind a closed industrial building. It was early spring and cold so we had the windows up and were playing music and laughing. A cop pulled up before we had the chance to do anything about it and ordered us out of the car. We were all 18, I believe, when the drinking age was 19 at the time. He asked for ID's and we provided them. With us was our friend and classmate John Thomas of Iron and his friend Larry, who didn't go to school with us but was a friend of John's. The policeman was looking at ID's and jotting down our names.

He got to Larry's ID, and upon seeing his last name, arched his eyebrows, looked at Larry with squinty eyes, and said, "Are you Sy's kid?"

"Yes sir," Larry replied.

"Dammit," the cop murmured. "All right, you guys pick up all the garbage in this ditch and get the hell out of here!"

I still was confused and not sure who Larry's dad was as I didn't really know him *or* his dad. After we got back in the car, Larry could see our confusion and told us that his dad worked for the sheriff's department or *was* the sheriff or something. Anyway, we caught a lucky break that time and were more careful when picking our drinking locations after that.

27. Cousin Buck

No memoir about Eveleth is complete without a story or two about my first cousin, Robert "Bucko" Kochevar. He's a legend for sure and he and his dad, my late Uncle Bobo Kochevar, could write books about themselves and the shenanigans they got into in Eveleth and elsewhere. I could write just about Buck and fill up a full book. Buck and I spent a lot of time together growing up. We lived a bike ride away and I liked his neighborhood better than mine as there were many more kids to play with than in mine. We fist fought almost every time we were together, gave each other plenty of bloody noses and bruises, but that was just regular Eveleth-stuff for most boys. He was the brother I never had and I'm sure he feels the same way about me. We were best men in each other's weddings too! We also lived together for two years in Bemidji while attending college.

There is one story that always comes to mind: It must have been around 1987 or 88. Buck, myself, and Gaylen Nelson, an Eveleth classmate of mine decided to go to Hibbing to see Buck's then girlfriend Maggie and hit a bar or two on Hibbing's classic main street. We spent a couple of hours there, bought a 12 pack of beer for the ride back and decided to hit the Eldorado in Virginia, then one of the best bars anywhere which had live music, fun Virginia girls, etc.

It was the dead of winter, probably -20 degrees, and one of those nights where the windows of the car were frosted up. Buck was on main street driving his blue Chevy Malibu. We approached the "Eldo" and he saw that there was a prime parking spot right in front of the bar. Now, this was during those years when the city of Virginia decided to have people park perpendicular to the street so making a U turn and driving straight into the spot seemed doable. Buck pulled a U turn and upon straightening out to get into the parking spot hit the corner of the parked car next to the open spot. Not usually a big problem but at that exact moment the Virginia main street beat cop was standing right there and saw it all! Buck panicked and took off. I was in the back seat enjoying a beer and I remember looking back and seeing the cop on his radio calling for help, I assumed. I told Buck to pull over or go back, or something. He wasn't listening. He raced down the main street toward Silver Lake, saw that the lights were red, so he took the short cut through the drive-up area of the corner liquor store (was it Rocket Liquor?) and kept on driving.

    Things like this never end well so Gaylen and I are preparing for the inevitable: we are trying to stuff the rest of the 12-pack under the seat, beers are rolling around the car, and we're being thrown about as the car didn't have any seat belts! Another block or two and there's a cop on our tail, then another one joins the chase and I'm thinking, Buck's screwed for sure. There might have also been some illegal plant substances in the car so those were properly secured where they wouldn't be found without a full body search or a proctologist.

    The next part I still find hard to believe. The chase ended, I remember, somewhere near the old Miners' Memorial hockey rink. Buck puts the car in park, grabs a winter cap, pulls it down low over his head, and gets out of the car to go talk to the two cops in their cars! Now, Gaylen and I are having a nervous discussion about car searches, nights in the city jail, and who might have to show they are sober enough to drive Buck's car back to Eveleth. We were expecting anytime for the cop to approach the car and search it.

About three minutes later, Buck opens the driver's side door, gets in, and says, "Ok, let's go."

Um……what!? He explained that he told the cops he was supposed to pick up his mom at the bar, didn't know he "nicked" the car, and promised to go back to the bar and figure out who owned the car he hit and get all that business straightened out. He never did, of course.

Now, Buck may have been a legend on the hockey rink, football field, and baseball diamond but I think his true talent was displayed right there on that cold winter night. He could charm his way out of the electric chair. The worst-case scenario could have been a DUI, open bottle, hit and run, evading police, leaving the scene of an accident, speeding, reckless driving, no seatbelts in the vehicle, and if they searched the car closely, God knows what else they would have found! He drove away with nothing but a smile and a great story to tell which, if our folks read this, are hearing it for the first time.

We didn't talk too much about that incident after but, in retrospect, the fact that it was -20 had a lot to do with it. The cops probably did not want to be outside of their cars freezing while doing their due diligence as if it was a weekend night in July, the outcome would probably have been much different.

28. "Nine Lives" Nartnik

No Eveleth book is complete without mention of our late friend Jimmy "Nine Lives" Nartnik or "Nartz" are we called him. Everyone has a crazy Nartz story. Jimmy lived life on the edge and looking back, he lived much like a rock star.

I knew Nartz in high school but didn't really travel much in the same circles until the two years after. I was attending Mesabi CC in Virginia when I ran into him there in the fall of 1986. His dad wanted him to take a few classes, learn accounting, and eventually take over the family blacktop business. I was in my second year there and had not seen much of him since he graduated one year ahead of me from Eveleth HS. We quickly got reacquainted and began to hang out frequently outside of school. He eventually started to pick me up on school mornings and sometimes brought me home because, as mentioned earlier, I didn't have my own wheels until a year or two later.

One ride home was quite memorable. He dropped me off on Jones Street about 2pm and drove home to find two FBI agents having coffee with his mom at the kitchen table. Jimmy got pinched in that car/truck stealing ring operating with a few older Evelethians which on that fateful day, all were arrested and hauled to court for arraignment in Virginia. Nartz was arraigned for knowingly buying a stolen pickup truck. He later said he was still wearing his school backpack when arraigned before the judge. Such a funny image.

Jimmy pleaded guilty, I believe, and received a few months of serving time with something called the Huber Law. It meant he was free to attend school and work but had to sleep at the city jail in Virginia.

He also was not allowed to drink if I remember right. Many times over those months, I brought him to the Virginia Police Department's holding cell where he slept. Sometimes, we'd get McDonald's or Hardee's first before I dropped him off. He hated it but the law's the law.

One weird and funny thing about his arraignment. He later told me that one of the FBI agents in the courtroom was "Breakdance Bill" wearing a suit and tie. If you had ever hung out in downtown Virginia during the year or two preceding, you knew Bill. He dressed like a homeless person and was always breakdancing on the main street. He used to wear a snowmobile suit when it was too warm to wear one. We thought he was just a street person. I suppose it does make sense, somewhat. This "Bill" guy might been in the area for a while investigating the auto theft ring. Being that many of the the stolen vehicles were brought to the Iron Range from out of state, it would definitely have been an FBI case. But, who knows? It might just be Nartz being Nartz. But then again, no one ever saw "Bill" again in Virginia.

I remember once or twice going out to his dad's business in the country near Sparta to hang out and have a few beers. He had his truck stored there and I could never quite understand why he never drove it. It became clear later that he was hiding it for a few months as he knew it was hot.

Later when I moved to the Twin Cities, I used to go see him as he had moved to Maple Grove and worked for the City of Maple Grove or Edina or somewhere for a year or two driving a grader or some heavy equipment. He also began raising Siberian Huskies in his fenced in yard. He'd sell them for a pretty good price too. I remember being impressed how he vetted these would be owners to make sure they had the adequate facilities and knew how to properly care for these type of dogs. He loved them. He used to pour full cans of Campbell's chicken soup into their dog food. Great memory.

At the time, I still had the car I got when I was 21, my dad's old 1984 Cutlass. It was pretty nice but, at times, undependable. I used to bring it to Jimmy's house in Maple Grove and he'd tune it up, change oil, and do whatever he could to help me make it last. Then I'd sometimes take him out for a few beers and dinner.

Now, while I live in Brooklyn Park, when I drive on highway 81 through Osseo, I still see the building where I bought the auto parts needed for my car when I was bringing it to his place for repair. It's not an auto parts store anymore but it's still a nice memory.

I last saw Nartz in front of Eggy's Bar after the 4th of July parade one year when a young girl, about 5, tugged on my shorts and said, "Jimmy wants to see you." I looked up and there he was. The girl was his girlfriend's daughter. We had a nice chat. Two or three weeks later, He was gone. He was working as an ironman building Bemidji State's new hockey arena and was found dead in his truck at the motel he was living at, a victim of a heart attack, I believe. I still think about him often.

29. Nonny's (Part Deux)

If you are of a certain age, you probably had your first bar drink at Nonny's Bar. I was a few years too young and Nonny's ceased to exist after the fire that also took with it my junior high hangout, Sib's pizza.

Every Evelethian knew or knew *of* "Nonny" Horoshak, Eveleth's version of Robin Hood. I knew him, kind of, from just being a bartender at the Elk's Club and seeing him around. My parents loved him and talked about him often. Nonny was a class of 1957 graduate from EHS.

One winter day in 1992, I was home hanging out alone. It was the one year I substitute taught on the Range and for some reason, I didn't get called in that day. I was also tending bar at the Roosevelt for the new owners whom the Delich family sold the bar to but was looking to move on from there but also working hard to find a teaching job in the Twin Cities.

The phone rang and it was Nonny. He told me that he was going to be managing Mugga's Bar (Formally Mr. Mitch's) and was looking for an afternoon bartender to start very soon. He seemed to know quite a bit about my bartending skills and I was recommended by someone as a good hire. He explained that the bar would be called Goodfella's and the new owner was Carver Richards (which I had heard.) I explained that I was substitute teaching almost every day so I wouldn't be available until after 3pm or later each day. He was fine with that as he needed a happy hour bartender who could cover the 3-7pm shift until the night shift person came in. It seemed to work well so I agreed to start in a week or two.

It ended up working much better as my dad's principal at the intermediate school in Biwabik (grades 6-8) asked me around that time to just work for him every day so I was done at 2:45pm every day and could get to the bar by 3pm.

So, I began showing up at Goodfella's at 3pm every weekday to cover those four-hour shifts.

Working for Nonny was interesting. He knew I had a few years' experience of pouring drinks so he mostly let me do my thing. He taught me a ton about how to get the best deals on liquor, how to ask salesman for the best deals based on how many cases bought, etc. and much more about managing a bar, etc. He even let me train a new bartender. These were all things I never had to deal with in my other bartending jobs but great information to know in case I ever thought about managing or owning a bar.

Working at a place on the highway was interesting as I met a lot of people you never saw downtown and many who just stopped on their way north or south on highway 53.

Nonny seemed to have several "visitors" who came in looking like cast members on the Goodfella's movie. They often sat at a quiet table and talked. Who knows what deals were going down? I felt like the character "Spider" from the movie who poured the drinks and served the sandwiches for the mob crew in the movie. Just hanging around but not really hearing what was going on. Or, pretending not to. It was quite an education. He even installed a one-way mirror in the back office by where the stage was so he could observe the happenings in the bar while doing his managing work. Nonny was always good to me in many ways and he often told me how much he loved my parents. I worked there for about five months or so before moving to the Twin Cities to teach that August.

Many years later, Nonny died on Lake Vermillion when his large snow plow fell through the ice when he was plowing roads for ice fisherman. He was quite a guy and I remember my parents being very sad that he was gone.

30. Winter (It Didn't Suck Then)

As a man approaching middle age, I hate winter. Yup. Hate it. First of all, the two things I love to do: Golf and putzing in my yard cannot be done with a foot of snow on the ground. I'm not an inside person. As a child in Eveleth, our winters were certainly longer than they are for someone like me now in the Twin Cities but I have great memories of winters in Eveleth.

First of all, the main reason for us being outside so much is that our parents did not want us inside. Eveleth kids in my day had to be busy. We did not have 200 channels on our television sets and certainly no video games. So, we went outside, sometimes in weather that was way too cold to be out there. Often in clothes that did not properly warm us. Not a problem. We never stopped moving.

The main things we did were skate and play hockey on the outdoor rinks. My main rink of choice was the one behind the Franklin School. This was the main one for a pickup game or just to shoot pucks. It had a nice wood burning stove in the warming shack that warmed us when we needed to be warmed. I can still smell the inside of the shack: a combination of sweat, body odor, heat, moldiness, and wet leather. We loved it. We honed our skills playing games for hours in the cold, warmed up when needed, and hardly thought about eating anything or going home.

My friends Ross Richards, Tommy Warn, Figgy Ritacco, Chris Spragg, and Scott McNulty and others used to play our share of boot hockey in the alleys behind our homes. That was always fun. Tommy's dad made or had made some goalie nets out of iron pipe so playing at his place was extra fun. It was just the net frames with no nets but it didn't matter. It was better than chunks of snow to mark the nets. We even named our own alley areas after famous NHL rinks. Mine was Maple Leaf Gardens in Toronto. I think we all named them after the cool teams, the original six NHL teams.

I also loved to build snow forts and tunnels in the snow. Northern Minnesota had a ton of snow. There never seemed to be a shortage to make forts and have snowball fights. My neighbor, John, and I used to gather a few friends and make a bunch of snowballs and throw them at cars from the alley or hidden behind the fence at the old office building across from the library on Pierce Street. Many times, we had to run for our lives if a car stopped and we thought we were seen.

Some years the snow was so high in the yard I could climb onto the garage roof and jump into the snow. Once, while jumping off the neighbor's roof, I ended up in a pile up to my neck and it took me quite a while to climb out. I didn't want to yell for help as my folks would have figured out that I jumped off the roof and I didn't want to lose the chance to do that again.

As I got older, I was able to hang with the Tusa boys and ride on their snowmobiles. They even had an extra one, I remember, so I got to go on some fun rides across St. Mary's Lake and around and over the many hills of the Eveleth Golf Course. They had a three-wheeler too and that was even more fun. Do they even sell three wheelers anymore? They were a bit tippy and have been replaced by the more stable four-wheelers years later.

We also ice fished but it was pretty cold out on the lakes and no one had an ice house or could afford those fancy personal shelters so that didn't last too long. Plus we fished all the time in the summer.

For a time, we had another fun winter activity. We called it "getting hookers." No, not that kind. This was sneaking up behind a car at a stop sign and grabbing the bumper and holding on for dear life as we rode a few blocks while being pulled behind. If you could stay on for a few blocks, that was bonus points. I think we might have even done it on the school buses a time or two. I always had the idea that grabbing hookers was the best way to get home from school each day instead of actually walking.

   I remember on the coldest afternoons in high school dreading the three-block walk home in -40 wind chill. I used to be able to catch a ride with someone going my way. Once, the Tusa brothers, in their old Country Squire station wagon, piled as many of us into it as they could. They were bringing the majority of the occupants to the Hippodrome for hockey practice. When we arrived there and unloaded, there were 18 of us that got out of the car! It was kind of the 80's version of filling phone booths, I suppose.

   Another great Tusa station wagon story: It was early spring and mild enough to have one of the first woods parties at Horseshoe Lake or wherever it was. There was still quite a bit of piled snow on the boulevard in front of my house on Jones Street. It was about 10pm and I had declined to go to this party. I must have been grounded or drunk the week before or something. There was a knock on the door and there was a wobbly Keith Tusa. He explained they were on their way to Virginia to get some food at McDonald's and needed a driver. Fine, I agreed. When I followed him outside, the station wagon was perched on top of the hard packed dirt-covered snow right in front of my house. It might have even had two wheels off the ground. Nice park job, Keith. I got in and there were a few others: Tommy Hilfers, Gaylen Nelson, and a couple of girls, one passed out in the back seat. So, after having to get pushed off the bank, I drove them to Virginia and back to the party. I'm not even sure I had my license at the time. Good times.

31. Taco John's

There was a Taco John's in Virginia that, I assume, made most of their money off the bar crowd at 1:15am. It was quite the tradition to hit the Virginia bars after starting in Eveleth. The main bars in Virginia in 1985 and 1986 were Willie's and The Eldorado. The "Eldo" was my favorite as they had a separate room with a smaller bar and live music on Fridays and Saturdays. We always ended up in Virginia as there were more people our age, more girls, more fun, etc. We used to start in Eveleth at Sleeve's or the Roosevelt at around 6pm. We knew the Eldo had two for one from 7-9pm so it was important to get in the car and get there by 8:45 so we could put in a two for one order which was often buying two beers so you could get four. Getting there by then was important if a good band was playing as we needed to get prime seating to see the band and the girls on the dance floor. Priorities!

    The good bands that played on a regular rotation were the Jackets and Trix. We used to yell, "Trix are for kids!" Trix were a three-piece band that played mostly 60's and even 50's like Carl Perkins and Elvis. They were awesome. Their guitarist was the best around and could handle the lead *and* rhythm by himself. They just killed on Beatles, Stones, and Who songs. My friend Jimmy Kennedy played there too a couple of times with bands he would put together for the summer.

    When we closed down the Eldorado, it was tradition to head to Taco John's to get some food and try to sober up. Our go-to meal was always two softshell tacos, their addicting potato oles, and a very large cup of ice-cold water. It was always important to make sure at night's end, you had a $5 bill left over for the trip to Taco John's. Nothing hit the spot after 1am than that and it usually helped steady us a bit to get home. If it was summer, I'd have to be at the golf course by 6am to mow the greens or change the cups or whatever. So, sleep was a luxury in those days.

32. Mr. P

Since I've had a long career as an elementary teacher, it's inevitable that many of my own memories as a student are shared with my students. I talk about Mr. Dick Paciotti quite often as he was one of my favorites and he taught me in 3rd grade and again in 5th grade. Those days were different, of course. The teachers could pull hair, cuff you across the head, and whatever they wanted to keep you in line. You were too afraid to tell a parent as you would get round two at home for misbehaving in school. It would have been even worse for me as my dad was a teacher and he would not have been happy to have me getting in trouble in school. It would be like being in a 10-round prize fight.

Mr. P was pretty young in those days, maybe around 30 or so. He had one of the best ways to get a child to pay attention. If he saw someone not looking at him or daydreaming, he calmly walked over and grabbed a chalkboard eraser, turned, and threw it as hard as he could at the kid. I remember he hardly missed. The best ones were when he hit someone in the forehead and left a chalk mark. It worked well, and kids usually paid attention. I don't remember ever getting one tossed at me but he did put me in the hall often when he got sick of me. Again, the ADHD didn't help my behavior and focus at all.

I still remember that he always wore white buttoned shirts and you could see his cigarette package in the breast pocket. He usually took a couple of smoke breaks a day. He'd tell us to do this page of math or read this chapter and he'd walk to the lounge and light up. I remember seeing the lounge door open and the smoke just billowing out from the staff in there having a smoke. It seemed everyone smoked in the 70's.

The children in my classes today are always amazed what the teachers did in those days, how they disciplined, etc. Things have certainly changed.

33. Go Carts (Helmets are for wimps)

I grew up across the alley from the Perushek family, as mentioned earlier. On the other side of them was the Hill family. Their oldest boy, Brian, was five years older than me and he let me hang out with him in the old barn the family had on the edge of their property.

Brian was one of those who could fix anything. He was always tinkering with something in the barn, which was more of a workshop/hang out area than anything. In the summer, I'd walk over there occasionally to see if Brian was around and see what project he was currently working on. He might have been working on a mini bike or, as was the rage then, building a go cart.

Later, Brian had built a motorized go cart but, before that, we built these basic go carts out of spare parts and plywood. They did not have engines. If someone was getting rid of an old gas lawn mower, we would ask for the wheels as they were the perfect size for the go carts we built. If the back wheels were bigger, it was cool looking like a muscle car. I didn't have too much of a talent for building things as a seven or eight-year-old but Brian was an accomplished mechanic at 12.

   When the rudimentary go carts were finished, we painted them, added a number on the side like the NASCAR cars, and took them to the nearest steep hill to race them. Rarely did these carts have a steering wheel. Those were hard to come by. Usually, they were steered with a rope.

   I started just tagging along with Brian to the steep hill in front of the Diggerness house on Jones Street. After making sure there were no cars coming, we jumped in, got a push, and raced down the steep hill. There were no brakes on these things so stopping was always a challenge. Avoiding parked cars, oncoming traffic, dogs, curbs, pedestrians, cops, and getting seriously injured was always a challenge too. I do remember some minor injuries like scraped knees, bumped heads, etc. but we tried to hide those from our parents so then we wouldn't have to admit what we were doing.

On my 10th birthday, July 31, 1976, I went to the Ely Lake beach to swim. Upon my return, I heard that there had been a fire at the Hill barn. Evidently, a match was dropped on the gasoline-soaked dirt floor and the whole place went up. Brian and another neighbor were inside. They got out with the help of next-door neighbor Charlie "Poosh" Perushek, who heard screaming and jumped the chain link fence, wrapped the boys in a rug and smothered the flames on them. Mark, Brian's friend, survived, but Brian, with horrible burns over much of his body, died a month later. He was 14 years old. Things were very different in the Jones Street and B Avenue area for a long time after. I never forgot that I could have been in that barn when this happened.

34. Golf, that Lost Wedge and Putter Head

My neighbor Tom Murphy in Brooklyn Park loves golf as I do. The one thing that irks him is playing with someone who can't control their emotions on the golf course. If he's playing in a club match at Edinburgh USA, he watches if his playing partner is having changes in emotion, such as anger at bad shots, or playing the whiny game of thinking the wind, grass, sand, etc. are playing against him. He uses that opportunity to turn the course of the match as an angry golfer gets frustrated easily and can sometimes be beaten easier.

I've only known him for about six years and he recently mentioned that he likes golfing with me because I'm so even keel out on the course. It's mostly true. I am now. But it wasn't always that way.

Growing up playing the Eveleth Golf Course was awesome. As mentioned earlier, I spent a lot of time out there working and golfing. I used to have much more of a temper while golfing. We often played for money and losing what little money we had was painful. Hitting a bad shot or missing a makeable putt often brought out anger and there were instances of club throwing, etc.

One Christmas I received a new putter. It was a Ping Anser putter, my all-time favorite and the putter my favorite golfer, Tom Watson. A couple of seasons later, after three putting the first three holes, I tossed my ball up in the air and swung at it like a baseball. I caught it solidly and the ball went into the woods followed by the head of my beloved Ping putter. It must have been loose from repeatedly banging it on the ground or on my bag after a missed money putt. I initially looked for it but could not find it in the woods. Many times over the course of the next few years, I would go into the woods looking for the head of that putter I missed so much. With the years of falling leaves and undergrowth piling up, I'm assuming it's still out there. Even today, every single time I putt on the third green in Eveleth, I look toward the woods and wonder where that putter head is. Probably buried under a foot or two of soil and rotting leaves by now.

The second "mishap" occurred several years later on the fourth hole. There used to be a large pine tree

in front of the left side of the green. I hit a chip and skulled it over the green. In my moment of anger, I threw the wedge up in the air with all my might. Unbelievably, it lodged in the branches on the very top of that pine tree,
which at the time, must have been 30 or 35 feet tall. It was quite a huge heave with the wedge and I was proud of the height I achieved on that thrown club. Unluckily for me, it didn't come down from the top branches. It didn't come down for several years!! Now, when it first happened, my friends had a long laugh at me when the club failed to come down. For many, many rounds after, I had to see my wedge on the top of that tree and was constantly reminded by my playing partners that it was still there.

    Many times when I had to change the cup on #4 or mow the green, I tried to knock it down with a chunk of wood or a rock and I failed. I can't remember if the wind finally blew it down or someone threw something at it but I later got it back. It was badly rusted and mostly unusable but it was one of many funny things that happened on the Eveleth course.

I never throw clubs now even though my neighbor and I do play often for money at Edinburgh or in Las Vegas. Clubs are just way too expensive now. I can usually suppress anger with some choice words or self-deprecating humor. Keeping an even emotional state on the golf course is important.

35. Winning it all at Target Center, 1993

The Eveleth hockey team won the small school hockey tournament in March of 1993 playing at Target Center. My uncle, Bobo Kochevar, was the head coach.

I was living in the Twin Cities and working my first year of teaching in White Bear Lake, Minnesota.

Eveleth won their first game on Thursday, which I attended. They were scheduled to play the semifinal on Friday afternoon at 2:30pm. I didn't get out of school then until around 4pm but wanted to see the game so I arranged for a co-worker to take my students for the last hour and went to the game.

In those days, Target Center had a bar in the lower level that was open during all their events.

Nowadays, there would be no alcohol in any venue during a high school event.

At the end of every period and before and after the game, the Eveleth fans ran quickly down to the basement level and had drinks. I remember running down the stairs or escalator as quickly as I could with my cousin Butch Mayasich. We were trying to get there before the rush of people trying to get a drink and claim a barstool before the rush.

Unbeknownst to me, my dad John and his high school buddy Gus Hendrickson had hatched a plan after Eveleth's first win on Thursday. Knowing the next game was at 2:30pm on Friday, they had an idea to get a venue close by and have a social for Eveleth hockey parents and fans after the semifinal game.

They talked to the manager at Gluek's which was right across First Avenue from the Target Center and found out that Gluek's had an open room on their top floor with a nice bar and tables.

The plan was that we would take admission to the event and donate all the money to the hockey team as a fundraiser. My dad asked that I go with him to get set up and serve as the admission collectors. I don't remember what we charged (maybe $5 a head?) but most people just made donations or threw a $20 down or whatever. I think several hundred dollars were raised for the team with this event.

The best and most memorable part was when my dad and I got over there a few minutes before the end of the game and set up a table to take the donations. There was a guy setting up the bar for the event. My dad, who was a bartender and bar manager for many years, knew some things about prepping for a party for Eveleth people.

He asks the bartender, "How many bartenders will you have?"

The bartender, with a puzzled look, replied, "Just me."

My dad looks at me, looks back at the guy, and delivers one of the best lines I've ever heard:

"I don't think you know what is going to happen here in a few minutes."

Knowing Eveleth, and thirsty Eveleth people, R. John knew, and he was right. About 30 minutes later, the place was swarming and the guy behind the bar had to scramble for more staff as the Evelethians descended on that room quickly and they were thirsty! I remember, being a bartender myself, how hard that was and spent time collecting glasses and trying to be a help to the staff. It was a great night as there were quite a few Eveleth people who lived in the Twin Cities that came by and it was a great reunion for them.

The next afternoon, Eveleth beat Lake of the Woods in overtime and brought their first state hockey title home since the early 1950's.

36. A Bottomless Pit

That was the name my dad gave to describe my unending appetite as a teenager. As many of us remember, we all looked malnourished because we never stopped moving and must have had incredible metabolisms. I don't think I was 145 pounds as a high school senior and probably didn't even get to 100 by 8th grade. But you'd never know by watching me eat.

During the years I worked at the golf course, we always had a "break time" around 9 or 9:30am each morning. Usually, you did your first job beginning at 6am or first light depending on the time of year. In those days, the only riding mower we had was the fairway mower or the "gang" mowers as we called them which were pulled by the old Toro tractor that "Yutch" Torrel kept going with duct tape and spare parts.

Anyway, we had walk behind mowers for everything else like the rough, tees, greens, etc. When I took my trip in 1985 to Scotland, the crew at St. Andrews had the same walk behind American made Jacobson brand greens' mowers that we had. That was cool.

So, what I'm getting at is all of us on the crew were skin and bones with all the walking, climbing, etc. as part of the job.

At break time, we'd head into the clubhouse or eat in the maintenance building after the new one was built. Coach Bill had a nice selection of donuts and rolls from the Italian Bakery. If they didn't get sold on the day he bought them, they would be two-for-one the next morning. If I timed it right, I could get four chocolate "long johns" for $2. I'd wash that down with a Pepsi and call it "breakfast." Now eating like that now in my 50's, I'd be pushing three bills in no time. Not a good look for anyone.

   Occasionally, my cousin Buck would call me up and ask if I wanted to go with him to Dan's Diner, the short-lived burger joint that was the old A&W on the old highway down from the cemetery. Dan had awesome half pound burgers and fries. The fries would come in their own bowl since the pile he gave us would not fit on the plate with the burger. This would be an easy meal for Buck and I. He also tipped the scales at about 140lbs as a senior.

   Once, I had just demolished a large Tombstone pizza at home. Cousin Buck called wanting to do a Dan's run. I told him I'd just eaten but would go with him anyway and shoot the bull for a while. Well, it didn't take long to smell the hot grease at Dan's and before you knew it, I had ordered and pounded down a half pound burger and a huge pile of yummy fries!

I could not gain weight if I tried in those days. I used to drink protein drinks when they first became available to try to put weight on for football but it was hard as I hardly ever sat down or stopped moving. I remember my mom buying Grandpa Tony those same protein drinks to help him put on weight as he was always so thin.

37. Winter Fun?

The very best sliding hill in the winter was at the Eveleth Golf Course. The top of the hill above the 9th green was great as it had a two-tier hill. You had a very steep one right away that flattened out when you slid across the green and then another steep one straight down before you ended up all the way to the base of the fairway. It was a long run that took a bit to finish. The only drawback was having to walk up two hills to do it again.

As a third-grade teacher, kids are always sharing with me what they did at their birthday parties or another party they attended. In the Twin Cities there are so many places you can go to have parties such as bowling alleys, gymnastics places, trampoline clubs, batting cages, mini golf, etc. I know I have hauled carloads of young girls to several of them when we had birthday parties for my three daughters.

In Eveleth, 40 or more years ago, the opportunities for these things didn't exist. Going to the sliding hill was one of the great ideas if you had a winter birthday. Sliding down the hill at the course for three hours was awesome and always a great party idea. Then going to the friend's house for a late lunch and cake was awesome. We loved it and we loved being outside.

During my kindergarten year, I went to one such party for my friend Rick Paoletti. "Ricky" we called him. He was later a linemate of mine in hockey before he moved to Virginia and played for the Blue Devils.

We spent a few hours sliding with friends on that day and toward the end of the time outside, I remember Rick's mom telling us that we only had time for about two more runs. We always knew that after you slid down the second hill, you had to climb back up on the outside ends of the hill as there was a blind spot just before the second hill and if you climbed back up the middle, you could get run over by a kid and a slide going very fast coming down.

Of course, I knew that and followed the rule on all of the many climbs back up the hill until it came to the end. Upon hearing that we only had a run or two left, I decided not to waste time walking to the outside edge and ran right up the middle to save time and maybe get *two* more runs in before we had to leave.

I was two thirds of the way back up toward the green when the birthday boy came out of nowhere. I had no time to move and he slammed into my legs, sending me flying "ass over tea kettle" whereby I flipped and landed headfirst into the snow with my left shoulder taking most of the force of the blow. It hurt a bit but, being a young Eveleth kid, I didn't cry and tried to show I was tough. That was the end of the sliding for me that day and we left shortly after.

After the party ended, I was home on Jones Street and my mom, noticed that I was standing in front of her with my left shoulder sagging down a bit. She asked why and I told her about the mishap on the sliding hill. She felt around my shoulder area and when she lifted my arm, I winced and said it hurt.

Being a nurse, she knew it was the collarbone. Off we went to the Eveleth Hospital and X-rays confirmed a broken left collarbone. I had to wear a sling for a few weeks which proved to be a pain as I write left-handed so trying to write with your arm in a sling was an inconvenience.

To this day, that collarbone was my only broken bone I've ever suffered. Pretty lucky, I guess, with all the hockey and football I played when being the one of the smaller kids on the ice and field not to mention the go cart races, bike jumping, tree climbing, cliff diving and other dangerous stuff we Eveleth kids did for years. I was always hoping to get a cast that others could sign in school.

38. Grandpa Tony and the $5 Bill Challenge

    This is one of my favorite memories of Grandpa Tony Boben. One day, my cousin Bucko and I had ridden our bikes down to see him and Grandma. We were probably seven or eight years old. Our sole purpose was probably to raid the big candy and gum bowl Grandma kept in the lower corner cabinet. We loaded up on that and Grandpa stopped us to ask a favor. I can't remember what he wanted us to do. It might have been to run an errand. I used to run to the old Koffee Kup on Grant Avenue to get cigarettes for him on occasion, so it might have been that or something else, like weed the garden or something.
    Anyway, the job was completed and Grandpa wanted to give us a bit of money. He opened up his wallet and realized that he didn't have enough $1 bills for each of us to get a couple so he took out a $5 bill and promptly tore it in half, giving each of us half of the bill, half of Lincoln's head and shoulders, and left us very confused.

Upon seeing the bewildering looks on our faces, he simply said, "Figure it out," and walked away.

Well, Bucko and I looked at each other and were not sure what to do. After a minute or so, we decided we needed to go to the bank and ask them if the bill was still good or not. We'd never seen someone tear up money.

We tore down to Miner's Bank on our bikes and presented the two halves of the Lincoln fiver to the teller and she scrunched up her face a bit. We explained what Grandpa did, she slid over her tape roll, taped it up, put it in her cash drawer and presented us each with two one-dollar bills and two quarters. We were rich! Without even batting an eye, we raced our bikes down to Buzzy's corner store on Fayal and bought orange push-ups and, presumably, more candy, pop, etc. That $2.50 went quite a long way in those days!

39. Mr. Mac

I had a lot of great teachers in Eveleth. As a teacher myself, you spend a lot of time in your training years thinking about teachers you've had and what made them successful.

One of my favorite teachers was Richard "Mr. Mac" McDonnel. I hoped I spelled that right. He was the art teacher at Eveleth Junior High. Mac, or "Mac Baby" like he was sometimes called, was a very funny guy. He looked like and acted like actor Dom DeLuise. He was always laughing, telling jokes, calling us "yellow bellies" and rarely getting angry. We looked forward to art class.

He was also a huge fan of the Beatles, often playing songs on his stereo. I was a member of his class in 8th grade and remember quite well the morning of December 9, 1980. It was a Tuesday. The previous night, during the Monday Night Football telecast, Howard Cossell broke that news that Beatle John Lennon had been shot and killed in New York City. My mom broke the news to me when I woke up and knowing well who John Lennon was and hearing it on the morning news, it was still shocking.

    My art class was second hour if I remember it right. Upon entering the room, the first thing I noticed was how quiet it was. There was no music playing and Mr. Mac could *not* be heard laughing and talking as we filed into the room. He was sitting in his desk quietly and looked to be drawing something. He did not give any directions and we just took that as a clue to start working on whatever project we were working on. The weird thing was that no one spoke. I think we all had heard the Lennon news and knew he was a huge Beatle fan so no one bothered to make a joke or be silly. We just sat and worked. Quietly. Very quietly.

    After a few minutes, I walked up to him and just said quietly, "Sorry Mac." I didn't have to explain why. He nodded but didn't speak. When I looked down at what he was doing, he had a picture of the four Beatles in front of him and he was drawing a target around Lennon's head. I'll never forget that. I also remember him being very quiet for most of the days until Christmas break. He was a very cool guy and one of the teachers I remember well but we sure felt bad for him that day. Later in 1981, we were constantly playing the new Stones cassette, "Tattoo You" loudly every day on his boombox. Mac would whine, "Jeez, you yellow bellies, the Stones again?"

40. Those Crazy Tusa Brothers

Most every group of Eveleth graduates has a Tusa story. Some of them go back into the early 70's with the older brothers Ed, Steve, and Doug. The twins, Keith and Kevan (there's that
-an again) were in my class and I spent more time than I should have with them throughout junior high and high school golfing and working at the Eveleth Golf Course.

To say the twins were crazy was not a misstatement. They were. It's a wonder that they are still among the living and don't seem to be affected much by past behaviors.

I could probably devote most of this book telling stories about them but two come to mind:

    An idea of fun for the twins was to explore their garage for any type of flammable liquid and fill a bucket with it. On Golf Course Road, where they lived, there was little traffic. Mostly just the neighborhood folks going by occasionally. They would pour the bucket of flammable liquids in a straight line on the road and light it. The spreading flame and line of fire was cool to watch, jump over, ride bikes through, etc.

    Once one of them was pouring the liquid and the other decided to light it early as the pouring was still going on. I think Gaylen Nelson, another neighbor of theirs, yelled at one of them to look out as the line of fire raced toward the other. Probably saved a huge explosion and possible injury.

    Another time, in April, the twins and Gaylen decided to take the Tusa's canoe and grab all the golf balls on the thin ice that were hit there in the spring and were there for the taking until the ice finally melted. I was in the car with my folks coming back from our monthly trip to Target in Duluth when, near the entrance from highway 53 to Golf Course Road, we saw an ambulance racing off the highway toward the course. I was thinking an elderly golfer had a heart attack or something but found out later those idiots tipped the canoe over and had gotten hypothermia from just a few minutes in the cold spring waters of St. Mary's Lake. I think a golfer saw them thrashing around and ran to call 911 and get a rope to get them out. Just another Tusa story.

Whenever we got "rained out" when working on the grounds' crew at the golf course, we went to the Tusa house and made egg and cheese sandwiches or just hung out until it stopped raining and we could get back to work.

One day, their mom, Jan, was there and said she'd make homemade French toast for the twins, myself, and Brad Windfeldt. She used at least a full loaf of bread, maybe part of a second loaf and we stuffed ourselves. Brad and I ate until we could not fit in another bite. I looked up and there was one piece left on the plate and we all knew it was the last one. I could see the twins eyeing each other as they chewed and I knew it was going to get interesting. Brad noticed the same thing and looked at me and nodded towards them. I think it was Kevan who swallowed his last bite and quickly reached his hand to grab that last piece. Keith could see that he was just a second too late, so as his brother reached toward the plate, he stabbed him in the hand with his fork! Kevan squealed, got up, and ran to the sink to wash his bleeding hand, swearing at his brother while Keith grinned and ate the last piece of French toast. Just another day in Tusa land.

41. August 16, 1977

The one thing about growing up in a small-town years ago was that it was safe and parents never worried about you. I'm sure they were smart enough to know we were tempting fate every day with riding bikes off ramps, swimming in mine pits, etc. but I don't remember my folks worrying too much. We learned independence as a young child. I feel sorry for the kids of today who are watched more and kept safe and close to home for obvious reasons.

This is why on that August day in 1977, having my mom, Shirley come looking for me was such a strange occurrence. My friend Ross Richards and I were playing golf next to the Eveleth Public Library on Pierce Street. We had been there a while when Ross looked up and said, "There's your mom."

I stood there dumbfounded as it was a shock for any adult having to come to look for us.

Sure enough, there was Shirley standing at the edge of the alley by the Olsons' house waving me over. I thought for sure that something was seriously wrong. Someone died for sure, I thought.

I walked over and could see that Mom had red eyes and she had been crying. Oh, crap, I thought, maybe one of my grandparents had died or someone was injured in a serious accident. As I approached her, she said softly, "Elvis died."

Now, I was only 11 years old but I knew who Elvis Presley was. My mom constantly played Elvis albums on the living room stereo. I heard them all the time and enjoyed them, both the early stuff and the "Fat Elvis" period material.

Shirley was an early Elvis fan, screaming in the movie theater when the *Love Me Tender* movie came out in 1956. She was 15 years old then and was one of the bobby sock-wearing Elvis fans going crazy for everything he did. She followed his career and loved him through all his movies in the 60's and his Vegas comeback in 1969 and into his last touring years of the 70's. Looking back on that memory helps make sense to me why she was so upset. I remember that she was not the same for weeks afterward and I tried hard not to upset her as she grieved for Mr. Presley. We played Elvis constantly in the months that followed as I'm sure many fans did.

Recently, my mom told me that she also loved Marlon Brando and saw *The Wild One* like 41 times!

She also likes Bob Dylan but only because he's Iron Range-bred and the same age as her and a fellow 1959 graduate. She often said, "Bob and I went to different high schools together."

42. Honestly, Officer, it Wasn't Me

My mornings as a golf course worker started incredibly early in Eveleth. Often, the crew got there before sunrise. It wasn't usually too much of a problem unless it was a Saturday or Sunday morning and you closed up the Eldorado at 1am a few hours before. Then sleep was a luxury.

I often was the first one at the course in the morning and one morning was remembered: The clubhouse had installed some kind of security system which must have been triggered by movement or something. I would imagine the technology in the 1980's was shaky as best. Now, as any of us workers knew, you never needed to enter the clubhouse to get to the mower shack. In the original clubhouse, the equipment was stored in the basement, a dark, dank, mouse-filled dungeon where we kept the tractor, the mowers, greens mowers, and other equipment. We didn't have the fancy equipment in those days.

The doors to this underground room were around the back of the building. If you were the first to arrive, you had to wait until the boss came to open up for us.

Anyway, I was there, the first one, and I laid down on the raised rock bed to catch a few winks before the rest of the guys got there. I heard a loud door slam and woke up. Thinking it was one of my coworkers, I awoke and ran up the bank to see who was coming. I then came face to face with an Eveleth cop with a large weapon. I remember it as some sort of fancy machine gun but it might have been a sawed off 12 gauge. He leveled the weapon at me and we both froze.

"Uh, I work here, sir," was all I could get out in my shaky, confused voice.

"The alarm was tripped," he replied and in his eyes, he seemed to recognize me and lowered the weapon.

"I heard that squirrels get in and can trip the alarm," I explained, and that was true.

"Ok, no problem," he replied, "I'll just go check it out." And that was the end of it. I heard the door slam and he left. By this time, one of the Tusa boys had arrived and was wondering why the police were there. I was too tired to explain.

Another time, I was sitting with my eyes closed waiting to start work when I heard a huge gun blast from the other side of the clubhouse. Shocked, I jumped up, and looked around. Here comes Scotty Spier around the corner carrying a shotgun and wearing a shit-eating grin. He had decided to take care of the crow problem we had. Coach McKenzie's wife, Carol, used to throw out pieces of old hot dog and hamburger buns for the birds to eat but all she attracted were crows. Now, if it's 5:30am and you are hung over and tired, the constant ca ca cawing of those stupid crows would wear on you and Scotty had had enough. We had a laugh about that and I remember suggesting we get rid of the dead crows before Carol arrived around 7am.

Still another time, I again, was catching a few 5:45am winks near the garage door when I heard what I thought was Andy Williams or one of the Tusas about to sneak up on me. If I remember right, it was like the morning of the third of July so I was probably out and drunk the night before.

"Anjj, I'm not in the mood," I muttered through the haze and headache.

No answer. I opened one eye and about 15 feet away was a spike buck and another antlerless deer.

They were as surprised as I was and as I sat up, they took off toward the 8th hole.

43. The "British Open?"

I've been a fan of the British Open since I went to Scotland to play golf in March of 1985. Only the Americans call it the "British Open." My friend Paul Martin is from Ireland and reminds me of this whenever I see him. The correct name is *The Open Championship.* The best part of this July tournament is that the weather is often windy and sometimes, wet. It's fun to see the pros have to play in this and hit shots they normally don't hit often.

My friend Andy Williams, who we called "Anjj," and I used to play a round of golf called the "British Open." It had to be windy and wet and often, we were on the course alone due to the weather. We used to start our rounds saying we were -4 and try to keep it under par as we played a nine-hole round in Eveleth.

Once we were playing this game in a misty, cool late summer afternoon. We got to the 8th hole and

Anjj drove the ball into the small swale on the side of the big hill about 185 yards from the pin. Anjj fired a nice driving 3-iron toward the green. It landed about 10 yards short and bounced up onto the green.

"Nice shot," I said, watching the ball roll toward the hole. We resumed our chat as we shouldered our bags and started the walk toward the green. I glanced up just in time to see Anjj's ball drop into the hole for an eagle 2. He did not see it as he was talking and looking at me.

"It's in," I reported."

"Really?" Anjj replied.

We had a nice laugh and probably a high five. It's always exciting to see someone hole a shot from so far out, especially in these wet conditions. It was one of the coolest shots I've ever seen.

"Anjj" was the golfer who shot one of the strangest rounds of golf I've ever heard someone play in Eveleth. He had a hole in one on #7, an eagle on #4, a birdie, a par, and some bigger numbers. He shot an even par 36 and had the ace, an eagle, a birdie, a couple of pars, a bogey or two, and a couple of bigger numbers. Probably the weirdest way to shoot even par in Eveleth.

    I have been playing this crazy game of golf for 48 years as of today and still play twice a week or so. I've still never have had a hole in one. Ever! Maybe I'm jinxing myself. Every time I get to a par three hole, I tell my playing partners that I've been playing this damn game for 48 or so years and have never had an ace. I've seen a few, including one at Esquagama CC in which my friend Pat Sjoberg got one on #9 using *my* 7 iron! He never lets me forget that. I recently saw one at my home course, Edinburgh USA. My playing partner, Steve, hit a nice five wood on the 185-yard hole and it took a hop and went in. It's always a thrill to see one live but I have to admit, I keep thinking I'm due soon.

44. That Blue Devil/Golden Bear Rivalry

Everyone who attended school in Eveleth or Virginia back in the day knows about the rivalry between our two high schools. Sometimes it extended off the ice or field and resulted in a lot of trouble making.

The Eveleth/Virginia hockey games were the best as the arena was packed for those games. I remember being hoarse from yelling at Virginia players/fans/the referees, etc.

Once, after Eveleth had lost to Virginia in the early 80's at the Hippodrome, some crazy Eveleth fan took a hockey stick and used it to shatter one of the windows on the Virginia team bus after the players were loaded on and ready to go home. The cop on duty at the arena grabbed the guy, and threw him roughly onto the nearest car (which happened to be my dad's new Dodge Omni) to cuff him. I'm not sure I've seen R. John angrier in my life. I was also amazed that someone could yell at a cop like that. I was very impressed. I'm not sure if the car was scratched or not as the stick-wielding crazy man was fighting back so cuffing him was not easy. I think some bystanders helped.

Another incident occurred when I was stick boy for the team in the late 70's. The Golden Bears had beaten Virginia at their rink. Now, everyone who played hockey in Eveleth knew that there was no wasting time in the locker room after the game when you played in Virginia. You got on the bus as fast as you could and headed home before there were problems. I remember the bus driver telling me they always took back roads out of Virginia as if they cruised the main street, there would be problems as our players would be flipping people off, mooning them, and agitating the bar patrons who might throw bottles, etc.

Anyway, we left the arena and headed down past Silver Lake near the convenience store across the street. Waiting for the bus was a small group of hoodlums who had broken into the outside ice machine and were armed and ready. The Eveleth players, of course, had the windows open in case they could yell at someone or have the chance to flip someone off on the way out of town. Those clowns unloaded handfuls of ice cubes from pretty close to the bus as the players ducked while calling them names, telling them they missed, etc. All I remember is the sound of ice hitting windows and the side of the bus. It was awesome. A great victory ride!

After my football team beat Virginia 27-0 in their homecoming game in the fall of 1984, we were chanting, "Main Street, Main Street" to try to get the bus driver to cruise the main drag so we could yell at Virginia people. He declined on Coach Sergeant's orders so that was a missed opportunity.

45. Making Money in Eveleth

All of us Eveleth guys grew up in a similar way. None of us had any money or for sure, any extra money. Before were old enough to legally get a real job, we had to find ways to earn money.

My first earnings came from shoveling snow for neighbors when I was about six or seven years old. I was lucky that we were one of only two or three families with school-aged kids on our block on Jones Street.

We had quite a few retired couples who needed some help with chores and sometimes, it even paid to do so. I started by just shoveling at the Skumatz and Marasco houses, and a couple of others. I liked being outside, even in the cold, and I had lots of energy. I would usually just shovel as a good neighbor for free, but eventually, I'd get a few bucks here and there when they noticed I was doing it regularly. It was a good neighborly thing to do which is very common in Eveleth.

On the end of the block was Reana Greenburg, who had a little black poodle named "Maedo." I used to walk Maedo often and Mrs. Greenburg always gave me a dollar or two which was great money in the 70's for candy, etc. She was a nice lady. Later, when I was in high school, she asked me to help her to move boxes for her move to wherever she was moving to. At the time, Reana was about 90 or 91 years old. Her sister, if I remember right, was also living there at that time so I helped move a bunch of boxes to a moving truck. Reana's sister was actually older than Reana but both of them had enough strength and energy to actually do all the packing and moving of the lighter boxes. They were both very tough women.

As mentioned earlier, I also used to do odd jobs for Mitch Batinich at his nightclub, called Mr. Mitch's. I would visit my dad down there when he tended bar in the summer and clean the parking lot or whatever for Mitch. I've always loved bars.

I also ran errands for Prim Skumatz when he was too old to want to leave his house and especially after his wife, Rose, died. I often jumped on my bike to get him cigarettes (as I also did for my Grandpa Tony) or pick up milk, or his pills, etc. He always appreciated it and gave me a couple of bucks once in a while. It's amazing that a young kid could buy cigarettes with just a note or a phone call to alert the counter person at the Koffee Kup that I was on my way. Only in Eveleth.

So there was always a little spending money to make before I started working for a regular paycheck at the golf course at 13 or 14.

46. Was I That Bad?

It should be noted that my kindergarten, 1st grade, 2nd grade, and 4th grade teachers all retired right after I was in their classes. True story. We never paid much attention to who was retiring and mostly, they kept it quiet. I don't remember them ever saying that this was their last year working as a teacher. I just remember them as old. When you came back to school in September, they would be gone.

This would have been the early to mid 1970's and many of the experienced teachers at the time, if they were women, didn't marry as if they did, they were not allowed to teach from a long-standing rule with the district. That rule was not in place by the time I started school but these four teachers obviously had started probably in the 1940's.

My kindergarten teacher, Miss Captanelli (sp?) was also my dad's teacher in like 1946 or whenever it was. I had Miss Dobbs for first grade. Miss Modec for second grade, and Miss Forte for 4th grade. Notice the "Miss" title? None were married. As mentioned earlier, Mr. Paciotti was my third and fifth grade teacher.

I never ever saw Forte or Dobbs ever again but used to visit Miss Modec in the nursing home. She lived to be like 103. She said she remembered me, which I believed as I was in her last class and it seems she might have remembered her last class. Plus, who could really forget my behavior?

Every year since I've been a teacher (32 years as of today) the school would host an open house so the kids could meet their new teacher, bring in supplies, see friends, pay fees, etc. This is usually done the week before Labor Day with the first day of school traditionally being the Tuesday after Labor Day.

Things were a bit different back in the day in Eveleth. We did not have an open house. You came to school on the first day and reported back to your previous year's classroom. The teacher often had cookies or something. You chatted about your summer, saw friends who you didn't see over the summer, and sat and waited to be told where you were going for the next year. It was always nerve-racking wondering who you were getting and which friends would be in your class. Also, it should be said that you never had to bring any supplies to school as that was always provided with the always adequate school funding in those days. I never ever carried a backpack to class until I was in college. I think in high school we had a few of our own notebooks, etc. but did not need much else. If I had homework, I just carried books, etc. under my arm. Things have certainly changed. Young students now have backpacks full of stuff their families have to buy for school and lug that backpack to and from every day. Even though I had a short walk to school for all my K-12 years, carrying a backpack would have been a pain, especially if I wanted to make snowballs to throw on the way or grab a car's back bumper for a quicker ride in the winter. I had priorities!

47. Grandpa Tony's Eggs

I love to cook and am able to cook many things if I need to. I was lucky. I was taught to cook at a young age from Grandma Mary and even Grandpa Tony. I always thought if a guy born in 1907 can cook, then all men should have at least a decent understanding how to put a good meal on the table. Sadly, many do not. As a parent of three daughters, I've tried to teach them that if they marry a guy who can't take care of himself, it will be like you have one more kid……a big kid. No one has time for that. This isn't 1950. Men need to man up and that means to share all domestic responsibility.

My mom, Shirley, is a great cook and always managed to get something on the table even after a ten-hour shift at the East Range Clinic. My dad also could cook, and even needed to at times before us kids were old enough to cook for ourselves safely. My sister and I learned to take care of ourselves, like many Eveleth kids, at a young age because our parents worked full time, helped out in their community, volunteered, helped their parents, etc.

One of the first things I learned how to cook was my Grandpa Tony's eggs. I must have been seven or eight at the time. Now, I think Grandpa was in love with lard. It seemed they always cooked with it. A chuck of that white fat would help to fry up many things like French toast, breaded walleye, etc. It was always good.

Grandpa would start by melting a huge chunk of lard or use the used lard they kept in the fridge. Sometimes he used bacon grease but had to add lard too. When it was done melting, it often ended up as a greasy, hot syrupy liquid an inch deep in the fry pan. He'd crack the eggs into it and they would actually float as they cooked! They would bubble and crackle and the edges would be dark and crispy on the outside. Add in the previously cooked bacon and some toast and that was breakfast at the Bobens. I'm still not sure how my guts could take that kind of cooking. It's a wonder I didn't just have the sports page handy for a quick bathroom trip right after I finished it.

That generation saved and reused everything. He used to cook up a half dozen polish sausages and keep the cooking water to use as a soup base. Genius. It already had the garlic and many other yummy things in it.

My mom taught me how to cook many things over the years, gave me tips on cooking certain things, shared recipes, etc. Even to this day, I love watching cooking shows on Netflix and shows that show food, culture, and cooking in faraway places.

48. The NBHA (The National Boot Hockey Association)

We all loved hockey in Eveleth and spent many hours playing games, practicing, playing pickup games at the Franklin Rink, watching North Star games on TV and generally thinking and breathing hockey when we weren't actually playing it.

On nights when we didn't have practice or a game, we often played boot hockey in the alleys behind our homes. We each had an area where we kept shoveled and played, sometimes with just one other person. We called these "goalie games." If I remember right, we might have had names for our boot hockey area. I'm pretty sure I called mine Maple Leaf Arena, home to the Toronto Maple Leaves. (Yes I did, it mentioned earlier) I think I just liked their jerseys. Most of the time, however, we had two on two or three on three games in the alley behind Tommy Warn's house. An added bonus was that his dad welded together a pair of regulation nets that we could set up instead of using found objects or snow chunks to define the goalie's nets. As soon as we had those to use, we never went to anyone's "boot hockey arena" other than the one at Warn's house so we could use the real nets.

During Christmas vacations, we spent hours playing boot hockey when we were not playing at the rink or practicing with our teams. We had some wild games, arguments, and the occasional fist fight when we couldn't get along. You know, regular Eveleth stuff. The regular crew for these games were myself, Ross Richards, Craig "Figgy" Ritacco, Scott McNulty, Chris Spragg and of course, Tommy Warn. So, we played three on three most of the time if all of us were ever to make it. We played with a real puck or sometimes if the snow was making the alley messy, a tennis ball. I loved boot hockey and even organized a game or two up in Bemidji during those college years.

49. Banned? Wait, I Work Here!

As mentioned earlier, I had many jobs in Eveleth with the golf course and bartending at three different fine drinking establishments. But there was an incident that almost got me banned from a place of employment.

I spent a few summers during college tending bar at the famous Roosevelt Bar in Eveleth during the Bob Delich years. I certainly could write several chapters of the goings on at the bar, the lessons I've learned, etc.

One weekend night during those years, I was on the fun side of the bar. The one that you could drink on, not that I couldn't have a drink or two while working. I had had a couple of drinks and was chatting with a couple of people while standing a few feet from the bar. Wouldn't you know it, the drink glass that held my cocktail slipped through my hands and fell to the hard floor, breaking with a loud crash. Everyone turned and looked at me and laughed. Whoops. Sorry. The bartender, Greg "Seve" Delich, made a disgusted face, but made me another. A couple of minutes later, I did it again. I dropped it on the floor and the glass splintered into a dozen pieces. Again, the laughing and finger pointing. Now the look Greg gave me this time was not as nice. He said something like, "Do you need a plastic glass?" He told me that I better hold on to the third one or he'll put me on the banned list.

"Banned?" I asked. "I work here."

"So?" he replied, "Anyone can be banned."

He was mostly right as we did actually have an unofficial list of a couple of people who were well known in town and were mostly unwelcome in many of the town's establishments because of unpredictable behavior when drunk. When I worked at the Elk's Club, I was made aware of one particular individual who was not to be served. It was only because he came up for dinner one Friday and I knew him well so he came to the bar and said hi. In fact, this guy was only allowed to drink in Virginia, the story goes, but who knows? I knew him and didn't think he was too much of a problem.

50. Can a Car Be a Hunting Weapon?

One of my favorite places up north is the land my Uncle Bobo Kochevar has maintained for decades at Long Lake south of Eveleth. This, of course, is not the Long Lake that is better known on the west side of highway 53 near highway 37. This is the smaller Long Lake, on the east side of highway 53 and a few miles south. You can get there by turning at Timber's Edge (it will always be Carolyn's to me) and taking that highway to a dirt road that leads to "Kochevar Bay." This Long Lake is a great walleye lake and the Kochevars have kept a trailer there for many years since Bobo's old man Willie begin leasing the land many years ago.

I had several chances to fish and stay out there as a kid with cousin Buck and Bobo and even more opportunities when Buck and I were old enough to drive and could get there alone or with girlfriends, friends, etc.

I was able to catch my first walleyes there with Bobo when I was pretty young. It was so much fun and a great memory.

When we got older, we used to go out there and drink a few in the old Airstream trailer that was handed down from Willie. It was a small and cozy, but a very cool place to hang out.

One incident is etched in my memory. I think Buck and I hatched the idea one summer afternoon after having a couple drinks downtown. We decided we were going to take a ride out there and dock fish or whatever.

When you turn off highway 53, you are on a two-lane county road for a few miles until you see the old Makinen store on your right. You turn there and take a very windy, hilly dirt road for a few more miles until it turns sharply left and you come to their road.

Anyway, that one night we are in Buck's Chevy Malibu, the one with no seatbelts, and were cruising down the dirt road, probably drinking beers when we came upon a deer in the road. This deer must have been a slow learner because rather than get scared of the car and noise and run into the ditch and woods, it just stared at us. Buck almost came to a complete stop before the deer decided he was going to move. Now, Cousin Buck never passes up an opportunity to "harvest" a deer, regardless of time of year.

     The deer, being probably the dumbest deer alive, takes off running not into the woods but rather straight down the dirt road away from us. Buck took this as a challenge and gunned the Malibu. The deer, bless its heart, did not want to veer off and go into the ditch and woods but rather kept running straight down the road with the Malibu on its heels. Buck is hooting and hollering like Bo Duke trying to run this thing down and have some tasty venison. I'm wide-eyed, holding on for dear life. We were able to get within a foot of the deer for the quarter mile or so that we chased it before the deer decided that it might get run over and took a sharp turn into the ditch and safety. We had a long laugh about that but it was pretty normal for Cousin Buck. Just another story he likes to tell.

51. Camp Chicagami

The word "Chicagami" means "camp by the lake." The legendary Camp Chicagami, located south of Eveleth on Pleasant Lake certainly fits the bill, being a camp by the lake.

I attended Camp Chicagami during the summers of 4th, 5th, and 6th grade, if I remember correctly.

I have not given my experiences of being a Chicagami camper much thought until very recently.

A former student of mine, Barrett Walker, recently contacted me about getting some volunteer hours in my classroom for one of his high school classes at Champlin Park High School. This is a common request as my school of employment is directly across the street from the high school. Barrett has an Iron Range connection, with his parents being from Biwabik. We got to talking when he visited and I asked him if he was working.

"Yes, I'm a camp counselor at a camp near your hometown of Eveleth," he told me. "Camp Chicagami."

Wow, I hadn't heard that name in quite a while. It seems, I learned from him, that the current Camp Chicagami is much more modernized now and it has turned into more of an overnight camp for the campers. A quick peek at their website showed me that it is, indeed, much nicer than the camp I remembered in the mid to late 1970's.

When I attended the camp it was more of a day camp although we had the choice to stay overnight on Thursdays with Friday being the last day of the week-long camp. I think I might have attended more than one week a summer but I can't remember for sure.

A few of the characters already mentioned in this book were also among the friends who I attended camp with during those summers. My cousin, Buck Kochevar, Pat Forte, the Kvaternik boys, Fritz and Kris (whose family cabin was right down the road)

Chandler Mohn (the son of our junior high principal) Richie and Glenn Mattson, and a few others made up our crew who attended camp at the same time.

I'm not really sure what goes on at the camp now but the website lists a bunch of fun activities like swimming, sports, crafts, hiking, etc.

In our day I remember a lot of swimming, softball, kickball, catching toads in the woods, not listening to the counselors, swearing, not being where we were supposed to be, purposely getting lost, stealing canoes and cruising the lake, fishing, visiting people we knew who lived on the lake, etc. It seems, especially when we were older campers, that the staff couldn't have cared less where we were or what we did if we returned by the time the bus left to return to town at around 3pm. Now, I'm sure the staff did care but not having to entertain a bunch of lippy 5th and 6th grade boys gave them a break in their day and they could concentrate on providing a fun experience for the younger kids while hoping our crew was not breaking too many laws or getting hurt in the woods or on the lake. Once we proved to them that we could make it back on time and in one piece, we were trusted to pretty much entertain ourselves.

    A typical day for our motley crew looked like this: We'd get off the bus, and tell the staff we were going fishing. We'd wander around the woods, building forts, taking out the canoes, smoking tightly rolled up brown paper bags like they were cigars, peeing anywhere we pleased, finding a few Lady Slipper flowers in the swampy wet areas, pulling them out of the ground(which we were yelled at for as it might have been unlawful)throwing the lifeguard's chair in the water, yelling obscenities at each other and strangers on the lake, mooning boaters, throwing each other's beach towels in the water, fighting with each other, climbing trees, going to the Kvaternik cabin, watching the college-aged female life guard in her bikini, wandering the nearby roads, throwing rocks at road signs and each other, tie dyeing our underwear, and generally acting like outlaws. No wonder the staff didn't want us around!

52. Who Needs Hearing?

I've always said that hearing is overrated. My dad lost his in his 50's and has worn hearing aids for 30 years at least. As mentioned earlier, he claims the damage was done by working the "waitress pit" at Mr. Mitch's nightclub in the 70's. The pit, where the barmaids filled their drink orders, was right by the stage at Mitch's and they had live bands most nights. He claims that now, with the hearing aids, it can work out to his advantage like when he doesn't want to hear my mom nagging him about something. He just turns them off.

I can tell mine are going on me. I'm at about the age when he first got his hearing aids. But mine was certainly lost in a different way.

I was at the age where wearing earphones (or buds like my daughters call them) with the old Sony Walkman in the 80's was trendy and I have always liked to listen to tunes too loudly in the car and when I walk the dog or am just hanging out and relaxing. It probably would not have been much of a problem but my choice of music (Stones, Beatles, Neil Young,

Dylan etc.) sound best when played very loud. In fact, a favorite Stones album from the late 60's had the instructions on the album to play it very loud. Blaming the bad hearing on the Walkman is only part of the problem. The main thing is that I've been around loud rock music since high school.

    My classmates, Rich Mattson and Russ Bergum, along with class of 86-ers Jimmy Kennedy and Timmy Leseman could also shoulder much of the blame. They had a band called The Imports while in high school. Now, live bands are loud in big rooms but the main problem was their practice space in the Leseman house in West Eveleth. It was, and I kid you not, the size of a walk-in-closet a good-sized house would have. When they practiced, Mike Hallstrom and I would get word of it and grab a six pack and go and hang out. There was barely space for the four musicians, let alone with two spectators. We would sit on folding chairs facing them and get the full force of the sound out of their amps as it practically made our hair get blown back and make us look like we were dogs with our heads out of the window.

I can't speak for Halsey but I'm sure we wouldn't have traded those times for anything. I credit the boys for fostering my love of music. Jimmy taught me rhythm guitar while we lived together in college. Rich has made music his life as he currently writes, performs, and produces other acts in his home studio in Sparta. Jimmy has a day job (musicians call them straight jobs) now but plays in bands on the side in the Twin Cities where he's a well-known "jack of all trades" on guitar, piano, and bass. Dr. Russ Bergum has also continued to play sometimes with Rich and also in the community orchestra in Rochester. I see Timmy on the 3rd and 4th of July and I'm sure he still bashes around on his drum kit. Great guys, all of them, and I still enjoy watching live music in bars around my home.

My current favorite live band is the Shag Band, with my friend Jill singing along with her two guitarists, both named Steve, who like Rich and Jimmy, have played together since high school and are around my age. I've gotten to know them well and try to make their gigs when I can. They laugh when I tell them they need more Stones and Neil

Young in their set but I think it's all up to Jill and what she wants to sing.

53. The Concussion Protocol: Who Needs It?

There is a ton of talk these days about the damage a concussion can be to an athlete or anyone who sustains a head injury. Athletes, in particular, need to go through what the team calls a "concussion protocol." I would imagine this is a battery of tests to see if the afflicted is thinking and seeing clearly before they are allowed to play, usually after a week but sometimes more.

As usual, Eveleth athletes suffered their share of concussions but I don't ever remember coaches even officially calling them "concussions." We usually just said the player "had his bell rung." Whatever that means. Sometimes, we just continued playing. Doc Martinson usually asked the player a few questions to see if they know where they were or what day it was or maybe he held up a couple of fingers and asked, "How many?"

I had two concussions for sure, and possibly three. The first occurred around 6th or 7th grade while playing hockey. I came home, vomited for a couple hours and after a visit from "Doc," he said I'd be fine in a few days. He was concerned enough, however, that he stayed, as I mentioned earlier, in our family's rec room and woke me every hour to make sure I didn't die in my sleep, which can be a concern with concussed patients.

My second, I assume, was in football. We were playing Virginia in 10th grade and I was playing corner and came upon my Virginia friend, Tim Anderson, the Virginia quarterback, as he came around the end on a keeper. I lowered my head toward his belt buckle and the last thing I remember is seeing him lower his blue helmet. My next memory is Coach McKenzie standing over me as I opened my eyes. Coach had this gold rain-type coat that they wore in those years but it looked blue to me. I remember thinking why is the Virginia coach coming to help me? I think I had briefly been knocked out. He helped me up and led me to the bench. I remained there as he thought I shouldn't go back in despite me saying I was fine. My future coach and now brother-in-law, Tom Lawrence, was at the game and came over. He was then playing football at UMD.

"You got rung up there, didn't you?" he asked. He looked in my eyes and said the pupils were dilated, a sign of concussion. I felt a tinge of pride as he had had his share of "getting his bell rung." I also made sure to ask if I had hit Tim hard enough to knock him down. I did.

A few years earlier, my cousin Buck and I were the regular "ball boys" for the Eveleth team as 4th and 5th graders and a year or two into junior high. It was a job we held for a few years until we played on the team. We had several jobs expected of us during practices and games but one job was strange and too frequent. If I player got his bell rung we were asked by Coach Dick Lawrence to bring the afflicted to the showers and assist them in getting their gear off and watching them until the coaches got there at the end of the game.

My brother-in-law Tom was a great player at Eveleth and later the UMD football captain. In high school, he played halfback and defensive back so he was doing his share of getting hit and giving hits. He was quite skinny then and usually absorbed the brunt of any tackle or hit. Because of this, he often got his own "bell rung." I seem to remember this happened at least twice during his senior year or maybe the year before too. One was particularly memorable. In fact, he probably doesn't remember much of it.

He got hit pretty hard on a play and needed some assistance getting to the sideline. His dad and Doc Martinson looked him over and told Buck and I to take him to the showers.

I remember Coach Dick grabbing me as I walked away and saying, "Get him in the showers but don't leave him alone." I wasn't quite sure what that meant at the time but I think Dick knew he was concussed and worrying that he would pass out in the shower and maybe falling and hitting his head again was a concern. He had obviously gotten hit badly enough that he was done for that game. Buck and I walked him past the Franklin School to the locker room. We assisted him in getting his pads off and walked him into the shower. I still remember his head under the water and him just standing there staring blankly ahead as the water poured down his face. We had to remind him to finish and watched as he toweled off and took a few minutes to dress, not saying anything. I think we ended up seeing his mom, Diane, shortly after who had come to check on him and she brought him home. I don't remember the word concussion ever being used and there certainly was no protocol as I'm sure he played the next week. Only in Eveleth.

Another time as a ball boy, in 1979, my neighbor, Stu Bradt got rung up big time on a kick return in Silver Bay. He sat on the bench and did a quick debriefing with Doc Martinson. Stu had no clue where he was, what the score was, what he did on the play, etc. It was a bit scary but he just sat out and had to be watched closely on the two-hour bus ride home.

My last time I remember getting my bell rung was my junior year of football. I was running scout team plays in practice and a lineman got too eager and leveled me from behind and my face mask went straight into the ground. I didn't seem too hurt but

Coach Kochevar, my uncle, said it looked scary. I finished practice, then later, proceeded to pass out into my spaghetti dinner at home.

My mom grabbed my hair and pulled me up. "You ok?" I told her I got hit pretty hard earlier. Shirley, with her years of nursing, just said she'd watch me and to tell her if I felt weird later. After a night of sleep, I was better and played the next game a few days later. Only in Eveleth.

My wife Traci and family have heard these stories before and know enough to keep an eye on me as middle age approaches. My sister always watches her husband Tom closely as he is now over 60 and has a longer history of concussions but he's a great shape now. We all know about the latest Mark Pavelich incident and head injuries are a real concern. I've told these stories to the gals at work and usually their response is something like, "That certainly explains a lot."

54. Jaws!

I was around nine years old in 1975 when the original *Jaws* movie came out. It was a great film and I think my mom, Shirley, counts it as one of her favorites.

Now, anyone with half a brain knows that sharks are ocean creatures and couldn't and wouldn't be found in Ely Lake or St. Mary's Lake. In the months that followed my repeated viewings of the movie, I was a bit freaked out when visiting my favorite swimming places, Ely Lake Beach and the areas near the golf course on St. Mary's. It was always in my thoughts that there might be a hungry shark in the waters when I was swimming at the beach or in the water looking for golf balls on St. Mary's.

In my present job teaching third graders, we study animal adaptability as part of our study of Life Science. I've talked to the kids about the bull shark, one of several shark species which can adapt to freshwater environments. Some have been spotted 2,000 miles from the coast in the Amazon River in South America.

There have even been sightings many miles up the Mississippi from New Orleans. I'm always careful mentioning that to my third graders as my school is only about a mile from the Mississippi and I don't want to freak out the kids, a few who live on the river or very near it and swim and play in it. Most have not seen *Jaws* and I usually don't tell them about it as I'm sure it would have the same effect on them as it did to me as a nine-year-old. I did, however, tell my own daughters this story many times and when they were younger, I'd take them to the beach often where I'd sneak up and grab their legs underwater like a human shark. Even underwater, I could hear them scream! Good times.

55. The Drunk and Stumble Corps

Years ago, when I was 13 or 14 years old, Eveleth had a pretty darn good Drum and Bugle Corps sponsored by the VFW. I heard about it and joined up not knowing what to expect. At the first practice, the only position left that were not filled by the older kids was on the rifle squad.

We were assigned old M1 rifles that had to be from the Vietnam War or possibly earlier. We were given a cartridge filled with blank shells and with the help and encouragement (mostly yelling) from "Czar" Vito, we learned how to march, shoulder the rifle, spin it around and make it look like we knew what we were doing and made a pretty respectful drill team.

The routines we had were pretty cool and the best part was shouldering and firing the rifle. It made a pretty loud sound and we could always see young kids on the parade route sticking their fingers in their ears.

We usually marched in about five or six parades over the summer, including, of course, Eveleth on the Fourth of July and Gilbert on the third. The Gilbert parade was always our favorite as by the time we were marching near the end of the parade, it was dusk and we could see the fire coming out of the rifles as we shot them. That was pretty cool.

I was part of the rifle team for two years and then, when it became available, switched to tenor drum, and during my last two years, snare drum.

Drumming well takes practice and we usually practiced a couple of times a week once school let out at the end of May. Scotty "Lippy" Wudenich was the main drum instructor. He didn't like when we called him "Lippy." I remember him saying, "You can call me Scott or Mr. Wudenich." Yeah, ok, Lippy. Whatever you say.

    We practiced by marching the streets near Monroe Park and if it was raining, we just jammed inside the old curling club building.

Our uniforms were pretty cool. We wore royal blue jump suits that looked like something a painter or a mechanic might wear to keep their clothes clean. We had spats over our while tennies, with the pant legs of the suits tucked into them. On our heads, a red beret. We looked a bit like we were part of some foreign military. It was an awesome look. We even had a VFW badge sewn into the jumpsuit. They were just like the ones on our youth hockey jerseys.

    Now, the marching, playing, and shooting was a big part of it but the most fun was the bus trips to out-of-town parades. I can't quite remember all the places we went but I'm sure we did the Water

Carnival parade in Hoyt Lakes, the July 2nd parade in Aurora and a handful of other city festival parades that fell on dates outside of the Fourth of July time. We were pretty busy in the summer.

One of the traditions for the new members was an initiation of sorts. Most were pretty mild like singing a song or doing something embarrassing. I was lucky. The head bugler was my neighbor, Scotty Bradt. I think he made me sing some stupid song on the bus. If the older guys thought any of the new guys were too young and/or lippy, the initiation became more unpleasant. I remember Scotty drawing long sideburns and a Fu Man Chu mustache on Terry "Skoog" Pernu with a permanent marker. He had to march with that on his face. That was super funny. He probably had that on his face for a few weeks after.

As I got older the bus trips took on a different pattern. We used to smuggle booze on the bus if we were lucky enough to have someone older who could buy it for us. The Tusa twins were usually the connection. We would often get root beer schnapps or sloe gin, or vodka. Usually something that mixed well with the cans of soda pop we were pretending we were drinking. I don't believe anyone ever got caught with booze but we certainly were buzzed up marching in a few parades. It was a fun memory and we actually were pretty good with all our marching routines...even under the influence. Did I mention we had a dance team of girls too? That always made it better!

56. You Better Swallow it, Devi

I was recently reminded of my high school classmate Kevin Devescovi. At my school parent/teacher conferences, I met the boyfriend of one of my students' moms. He had a very cool Hamm's Beer cap on. Of course, being from Eveleth, that would certainly spark a conversation. I found out he was not from Eveleth or the Iron Range but had relatives in Sparta. He asked if I knew his uncle, Kevin Devescovi. Damn right I do! I graduated with him, played football with him, and even attended Bemidji State University with him and occasionally hung out in a bar he worked at called Bottoms Up in downtown Bemidji. Bottoms Up was kind of a dance/nightclub type place and not my usual kind of place but I did go once in a while to see him and say hi.

      Anyway, it made me think of one of my favorite stories from my senior year. I was sitting in my Minnesota Ecology class with one of my favorite teachers ever, Mr. Bob Kesti. Great guy. If you remember Kesti's biology classroom, it had a full bank of windows looking out to the parking lot toward the Industrial Arts building. I was daydreaming (as usual) and noticed Devi's truck pull up. We called him "Devi" as that was the nickname Mr. Kesti gave him so it stuck. It's pronounced D*a-vee*. As Kevin got out of his pickup truck, he slightly bent over, stuck a finger into his bottom lip and scraped out the Copenhagen chew he had in his mouth. After a couple spits to clean out his mouth, he grabbed his backpack and proceeded to walk toward the entrance. I chuckled to myself and looked up just in time to see Mr. Kesti watching what I was watching. Now, I believe this was in the winter and Kevin played hockey. In fact, he was the best player, having moved to Eveleth from Gilbert to play hockey for a better team for his junior and senior years.

By this time, several of the students in the class were watching this unfold and watching Kesti watch it too. Of course, we thought Kevin was toast as far as being an athlete and consuming a tobacco product on school grounds. This was not going to be good. Anyway, I can't quite remember if Kevin had the ecology class or was headed to another classroom. I don't believe anything happened as Kesti must have given him a pass on this particular incident.

Another Bob Kesti chew-related incident was told to me by my friend and fellow golf course worker, Andy "Anjj" Williams. He told me that Kesti once saw an athlete with a mouth full of chew and told him he could swallow it or he would turn him in. Swallowing Copenhagen was not good and usually resulting in someone turning a few shades of green and vomiting. Kesti got the last laugh at that one.

Chew was consumed by many of my friends during those years. Kevan Tusa used to chew right in

11th grade English class with Ms. Anderson. She always had a ton of different magazines on shelves in her class. Kevin sat next to one of shelves and when she was not looking, he would grab one, open it up, spit in it, and close it. I suppose, by the end of the year, she must have had quite a few magazines with smelly chew spit residue inside them! Another short-lived craze was "sniffing snuff," a strong tobacco product we snorted, sometimes in class. It was especially easy in a math class where the teacher had his/her back tuned all the time writing on the chalkboard. The nasty stuff sometimes made me and others sneeze so it wasn't unusual to have half the class sneezing and weezing and have the teacher turn around with a confused look.

57. Grandpa Tony

My grandfather Tony died in December, 1995, and I don't think a week goes by when I don't think of him. As I get older, I recognize myself getting more like him. He was quiet. That was strange as his daughters Shirley and Annette never stop talking.

I'd like to live a long life but not one with bad health or needing to be taken care of to continue living. Tony lived to be 88 years old and never needed to be looked after. He drove his vehicle right up until his death and kept as active as he could. I think my mom told me that he actually worked on his last day on Earth. He had done quite a bit of volunteer work at the Eveleth Hospital which by the 1990's, was a nursing home residence. I'm guessing that quite a few of the residents were younger than him and he knew many of them personally.

Grandpa Tony came to visit my mom for coffee every morning at about 5am. My mom would usually leave for her nursing job by 6:30am so they had their daily visit each morning. I sat and had breakfast many mornings with him and heard the old stories and jokes.

Certainly, living to 88 is quite an accomplishment. I think it was even a more amazing accomplishment for Tony. He had some rough years with alcoholism during the 50's and early 60's. My mom and aunt had to endure this for much of their adolescence. It's a great tribute to them that they have survived this upbringing and led successful lives themselves. There were no Al-Anon classes for families of alcoholics in those days. My mom and aunt had to grow up quickly and there was hardly any money to go around. My mom has told stories of having to walk downtown from South Court to get Grandpa's vehicle so he wouldn't try to drive after drinking. This was often when she was 13 or 14 years old. She basically had to teach herself to drive. Grandma Mary never learned to drive.

  Tony was born in Aurora and was quite the legend there. Once, during my first week as a bartender at the Roosevelt Bar in 1987 or so, I met a retired regular during the day shift. I asked him if he was from Eveleth originally.

  "I was born and raised in Aurora," he told me.

  I thought quickly that he must have been around Tony's age.

  "Do you remember Tony Boben?" I asked.

"Do *you* know Tony Boben?" he replied wide eyed.

"He's my grandfather," I shared.

He smiled and told me that Tony was quite the fighter back in the day. He was only about 130 pounds as an old timer and probably not much more back then. Evidently, Grandpa Tony would get several drinks in him and basically pick fights in the bar. But he would always find the biggest guy he could find.

"Your grandfather fought everyone who wanted to, they were always much bigger, and he almost always won," the guy shared.

This didn't surprise me. My gentle quiet grandfather was always scrappy and thin but strong, even in his 70's and early 80's. My cousin Buck and I spent a lot of time with him and I remember his biceps were big and round even if he was slightly built. We used to grab them and try to squeeze as hard as we could. He never flinched. He just laughed.

His stories were always interesting and I find myself telling stories about Tony to my third graders. I probably talk about him more than anyone.

One story I remember well: In the 1930's, during the Great Depression, many miners were unemployed and struggling. President Franklin D. Roosevelt started the Civilian Conservation Corps (CCC) to give young men jobs and Tony signed up. He was born in 1907 so he must have been in his mid to late 20's at the time. Maybe a bit older.

One of the main work crews he was on worked up near Ely and the Boundary Waters clearing land for campsites, etc. They were digging with shovels into a large mound to level it and clear the land a bit. They found out that his large mound was actually an old Indian burial mound when they found bones. Quite a few of them. They quickly figured out what they found and it caused quite a bit of trouble as they had to get consultation from local Native Americans on how to proceed with the project, and possibly move the skeletons for reburial, etc. He said he never forgot that.

I remember one time around 1970 or 71. I went with my mom to the hospital. I'm thinking it was Hibbing but it might not have been. We were visiting Grandpa there. I was confused as to why as he didn't seem to be sick or recovering from surgery or anything. I found out much later that he had had a relapse with the booze and was drying out for a few days and getting the help he needed. I remember him saying that he quit booze cold turkey when his first grandchild, my cousin Laurie, was born in 1963. He never went back to the booze except for the one relapse and it probably saved his life.

Grandpa taught me many things. I learned some of my first cooking lessons from him (as mentioned earlier) and I helped him in his yard and garden. I still love planting vegetables at my home each spring and probably learned many of these skills from him. I'm proud to be his grandson.

58. Who's Driving This Boat?

It was late June of 1995. The class of 1985 was about to have its 10th Year Reunion. A couple of months earlier, a few of us, the Tusa twins, Chris Spragg, Lyle Johnson ('87) and Jimmy Luke ('86) decided we would make a week of it and spend a few days on one of those Lake Vermillion houseboats that you could rent by the day.

We had visions of fishing, cruising, drinking, catching some warm sun, and just hanging out for three nights and almost four days. We decided on the size that would work for us, what we could afford and booked it for a Tuesday-Friday tour so some of us could still make the Friday class reunion.

Keith Tusa and I planned to drive up from the Twin Cities on Tuesday afternoon after he got off work and the rest would join us later that night. Keith and I got to the boat place, filled out the required paperwork, and got our houseboat. It was a nice sun-filled day and Keith and I had several hours to cruise around, fish a bit, drink, and explore Lake Vermillion. No one had a cell phone in those days so we had a set time to meet the rest of the guys at the boat launch at Bayview Lodge later that night.

After a fun filled day on the lake, Keith and I, a bit buzzed and slightly sunburned, met the guys at the launch at around 10pm that evening. We heard them before we saw them. They had indulged in a few cocktails on the way up from the cities and were in a jovial mood. It was quite the contrast to Keith and me as we already had been drinking for several hours.

For safety reasons, the houseboat came with a midsized boat and motor attached to the rear of the houseboat for like if there was a fire onboard, etc. The late arrivals, who were still wide awake and in a party mood, spent several hours awake, singing, causing trouble, sliding off the slide attached to the top of the houseboat, and essentially did their best to keep Keith and I awake well into the night. Lyle jumped into the small boat, pulled the starting cord and spent the next 30 minutes doing circles around the houseboat with a beer in his hand while everyone laughed and egged him on. The waves he made caused the houseboat to rock a bit as we petered along.

One of the important things we had to do as part of the rental was to radio into the houseboat place staff and give them the location we would park for the night. If we forgot, they would radio in and ask us where we were before they left for the night. We were given a map of the lake with numbered locations and mostly, just gave them a number from the map whether it was the right one or the wrong one. I mean, did it matter?

Eventually, we got tired and settled into the bunks for the night as we had two and a half days remaining on this trip and were quite drunk. Before we did this, we'd have to park the houseboat for the night (and radio in of course.)

Early the next morning, I woke up first and seeing that everyone was still sleeping off the night before, decided to start up the houseboat and begin cruising the lake. I had only three or four hours of sleep but was excited to get moving. I poured a nice vodka/cranberry for breakfast and settled into the captain's seat. I started up the houseboat and with the map in front of me, begin to cruise. Jimmy woke up and came in to see me. We looked at the map and decided the route we would take. We had stopped for the night in one of the many areas of Lake Vermillion that was still void of cabins and houses and I set the course and headed out with some good old George Jones and Merle Haggard booming out of the large "boom box" I brought with me. I had also, a couple of days earlier, took an old pillowcase, tore it into a larger sheet and drew a large "pirate" flag with a skull and crossbones on it. We were certainly a motley crew now.

    Being extremely tired, I soon fell asleep sitting right in the captain's chair and spilled my drink all over my lap. This woke me up so I poured a new drink and sat back down to continue. The boat was going very slow so we could get up and walk around a bit without an issue. A while later, I fell asleep again, spilling the drink a second time on my already wet shorts. Now I realized that maybe I was not the best one to take the steering wheel if I kept falling asleep every few minutes. Everyone else was still passed out in their bunks so no one was volunteering to drive the boat.

I woke Jimmy and explained my dilemma. He agreed to take the wheel instead of us just beaching it again. So I went back to a much-needed sleep.

The three days and nights went by uneventfully other than it being about 60 degrees and raining most of the time. We didn't fish much but had a lot of fun and had a lot of stories to tell.

59. My Uncles

Earlier in these pages, I made mention that I am lucky to have the coolest uncles and I'm very proud of that. I have only one uncle from birth, my Uncle Bill Intihar, who lives in Albert Lea, MN. The other two, my uncles from marriage, have always gone by nicknames: "Demo" Mayasich and "Bobo" Kochevar. Demo's real name is Jim. I've never ever called him "Uncle Jim." Bobo's really name is Robert. I've never called him Robert or Bob. Weird, I know, but that's Eveleth. I bet you could probably think of a couple of people who go by nicknames and you don't know or can't remember their given names.

I'm lucky that, for the exception of Uncle Bill's family in Albert Lea, all of my relatives were born, raised, and lived in Eveleth. I got to see them all the time, not just on holidays.

Bobo had been a resident of the Eveleth Nursing Home or whatever it's called now. I used to go visit him every time I came to Eveleth. He had dementia but he never ever failed to greet me by my name when I walked into his room. Even if it's been several months since I last visited him.

Bobo, being a coach at Eveleth High School for many years, was a huge influence on me in more ways than sports. He introduced me to fishing at Long Lake, eating pickled northern pike and hot carrots he canned, and along with my dad and cousin Buck, introduced me to small game hunting at the Kochevar "farm" south of Eveleth. Most of all, he was my sixth-grade teacher! I used the memories of being in his class to form my teaching style, always expecting a lot out of the kids but giving them the support they needed to be successful. I even was his substitute teacher a few times.

As many know, Bobo was a runner for many years. He ran every morning before work and built up his endurance enough to be able to run in a few Grandma's Marathons in Duluth. My favorite story of Bobo running a marathon in Duluth was, once, after finishing the race, he went into a bar, ordered a beer, and sat on the curb drinking it and smoking a cigarette. I'm guessing not too many marathon runners did that post race!

Demo was also a great influence. I also found myself substitute teaching in Demo's room quite a bit. It was also his last year of teaching. Imagine that, there were four sixth grade teachers in Eveleth at the time and two of them were my uncles! I didn't see Demo as much as a youngster but, in college, I tended bar with him quite a bit at the Elks Club. That was a lot of fun. Demo played golf and I probably played a few hundred rounds of golf with him in Eveleth and around the twin cities later with my cousin Butch and my dad. We even played the "Iron Ranger" scramble at Hiawatha in Minneapolis for several years. Demo had an awesome short game and putting stroke. He could, years ago, shoot even par in Eveleth as he knew how to keep the ball in play and manage his way around the course. The old saying used by many was to yell "Demo" really loud when your tee ball was headed to the woods. This often got you a nice "Demo bounce" and you found your ball in the fairway. I still do that!

Obviously, I did not see Uncle Bill as often but we shared a lot of similarities. He had thick hair like mine, was lefthanded like me, and loved golf. He also played a ton of tennis and as a high schooler, played drums in a rock band. I was fascinated that Uncle Bill smoked a pipe and watching him load it up with sweet smelling pipe tobacco was pretty cool. Pipe smoking smelled so much better than cigarettes or cigars. One thing I've always found fascinating about my aunts and uncles was, every one of them married their high school sweethearts. My parents, too, dated in high school. I tell that story to friends and they, too, think it's pretty cool.

60. Rain Stopped?.......Let's Play!

I worked at the Eveleth Golf Course on their grounds crew from the time I was 13 until I was done with college, the last two years serving as "foreman" which meant not much more than saying I was one of the oldest on the crew and had the most experience. I think the foreman got a dollar an hour more in pay. A golf course is the best place to grow up and we were very lucky to have a steady job with unlimited hours and a chance to play a lot of golf.

As mentioned earlier, a whole book could be devoted to the shenanigans of spending the summer of my teens and early 20's mowing greens, changing cups and tees, mowing rough, dumping garbage, cutting trees, raking bunkers, etc. We did all of this without the modern conveniences of riding mowers although, when I moved to the Twin Cities to teach, the riding mowers suddenly appeared after many years of the city saying they couldn't afford them or the greens were too small and elevated to effectively turn a riding greens' mower around safely. All this seemed moot when the city assigned the course maintenance jobs to their regular city crew sometime after I left. With a much smaller crew, the riding mowers were a must. We had as many as 11 or 12 kids on the crew from the years I worked: 1980-1991.

Golf course maintenance has improved drastically in the years since. I now belong and live on Edinburgh USA in Brooklyn Park and observing their crews with the modernized equipment makes me wish we had that opportunity years ago. They even have a machine called a "Sand Pro" which is a riding machine that rakes the many bunkers at Edinburgh. When I traveled to St. Andrew's in Scotland in 1985 to play golf, I saw large crews of young kids with rakes walking the course and hand raking the dozens of deep bunkers on the course. No Sand pros then, and I'm certain, with the history of the course and the abundance of very deep bunkers, maybe not now either.

Eveleth Golf Course was hallowed ground and very unique. One of the strangest things is that the course was built on a soil called sandy loam. It's a soil/sand mixture that drains very well. It had almost a brownish-gold color and a weird consistency that was not like regular black dirt. It was gritty yet smooth and did not make your hands muddy when wet.

One time, during my last years on the course, I came into the clubhouse and Carol McKenzie, the wife of my golf coach Bill, said there was a piece of mail for me. It was from the University of Minnesota's agricultural or turf management division asking us to send a soil sample to them for a study they were doing on Minnesota golf courses. So, I took a piece of copper pipe, sunk it into the practice green and sent the "plug" down to the "U." I totally forgot about it when a few weeks later, Carol said someone had called asking to speak to the "greenskeeper." I called the guy back and he started by complimenting me on the strong root system the sample had and said he noticed that the top of the plug had good grass growth but had a question to ask.

"How do you grow grass on this sandy loam soil which seems almost completely void of any nutrients?" he asked.

"It drains well," I replied, not sure how to answer.

"What kind of fertilizer program are you on up there?"

"Uh, not sure." I answered. "We don't really have a regular fertilizer program in place."

"Ok, I have connections to the Toro company and I'll have them get in touch with you," he said.

I hung up, shrugged, and didn't really think too much of what he said. He did say the root system was good and we knew the turf looked good at the time, especially the greens.

We did have quite a few bags of unused fertilizer packed into a small room in the basement of the clubhouse where we stored all the equipment. We used to sit on them when we ate lunch but as far as applying them, we didn't really need to do much or know which ones to put on and when. We really were only concerned about the greens and keeping them growing and weed-free was always a priority.

I can remember, a few years earlier, Doug Tusa and Stu Bradt would fertilize the greens once every few weeks with whatever mystery bag they chose and it seemed to work ok. At times, they would go to the course after the bars closed at 1am and drive the course applying the fertilizer when the dew was on the greens so you could better see the wheel tracks and know where you applied it. Sometimes when I was out changing the cups a few hours later, and seeing the crooked lines on the greens, I knew they must had had a few drinks before they came out to apply the fertilizer. Only in Eveleth. I don't remember ever meeting with any fertilizer company but I'm sure it happened as the course has been in excellent shape now for quite a long time.

The sandy loam provided Eveleth golfers with an added bonus. When we had a heavy rain or downpour, the course always drained quickly and you could play as soon as the rain stopped whereas in Virginia, with its low areas and swampy turf in spots, would have to close for a day to allow it to drain. Virginia has since undergone a major rerouting and expanded their ponds to allow for better drainage.

61. Work Clothes-Courtesy of the USMC

    As mentioned earlier, my Grandpa Rudy and his brothers worked in construction and stone masonry and were responsible for quite a few chimneys and brick homes in Eveleth. My dad once told me that the cool stone wall that separated the football field from the lower baseball diamond and Franklin School hockey rink was something that their crew did many years ago.

    My dad grew up on Douglas Avenue in a home right across the alley from the house my Uncle Demo Mayasich now lives in. In the mid 1950's, my grandfather built that house for his daughter, my Aunt Mary Ann, and Demo to live in after they married. It was a cool brick house that, according to my dad, my grandfather pretty much built on his own. My dad used to help mix the cement and carry the bricks and serve as his assistant in the project.

A funny story from that time: My dad's best friend at the time was Lou (Sonny) Karakas, hockey goalie extraordinaire and all-around great guy. Sonny was over visiting my dad as he worked with my grandfather. They were messing around, as young teens usually did. I think my dad was chasing Sonny across the newly constructed roof and Sonny stepped through in a soft spot and his leg went through it. My grandfather just about had a shit fit and started yelling at them. Sonny did not stick around and pretty much took off running for home, not wanting to be around for the wrath of Rudy. It was quite some time before he ever came back to see my dad at home and I'm sure my dad was in trouble for quite some time too.

Later, when my dad was in the Marine Corps, he was stationed at a huge supply depot in the desert in Barstow, California. He had free reign to many supplies and clothing and Grandpa Rudy and his brothers did their construction work in Marine boots and fatigues for many years thereafter.

62. The Legend Called Bobo

The one thing that's weird about writing this book is that people I wrote about earlier as living humans pass away and that requires some rewrites, changes, or additions. I've spent almost six years banging away at this and it's bound to happen.

My uncle, Bobo Kochevar, passed away on May 29, 2020 exactly a month into his 84th year. He was certainly a legend to hundreds of Eveleth students and athletes as a teacher at the Franklin Elementary and coach of three sports at the high school.

I have so many memories of the craziness that was Bobo that I could probably devote dozens of pages to just him.

Bobo was my 6th grade teacher. It was a weird thing to have your uncle as a teacher. There were four teachers in the 6th grade that year and two of them were my uncles. "Demo" Mayasich being the other. I bet you could scour the world over and not find anyone who has uncles nicknamed Demo and Bobo or that they comprised half of the sixth-grade team in the fall of 1978.

My first and earliest memories of Bobo were fishing at Long Lake south of Eveleth in Makinen. This Long Lake is not to be confused with the one a couple of miles north on the western side of highway 53. This Long Lake was smaller and more desolate with not many cabins, few year-round homes, etc. It was where I did my first fishing from a boat. I caught my first walleye and my first northern there in a boat with Bobo and my cousin Buck and developed an early love of fishing.

A couple of times a summer, Bobo would take Buck and I out to fish and stay overnight at the small Airstream trailer he had on land first leased by Willie Kochevar, Bobo's dad. I was fun to have a fire, fish off the dock for crappies, roast hotdogs, eat chips and sometimes, have a little beer as long as we never told our mothers.

A fun memory is when Bobo would take Buck and I, probably about seven or eight years old at the time, on a night walk out to the main gravel road. I was never sure the purpose other than to scare the bejesus out of us. Now, you have to visualize this: There were no lights on this road, no city lights close by, and usually, all we had was a small flashlight that Bobo carried. It was pitch black out there. You could not see the hand in front of your face. We would walk behind Bobo as he led the way with his flashlight out ahead. The stillness only broken by owls hooting, rustling of grass and weeds in the ditches, and the occasional firefly which Buck and I always tried to catch.

It never failed, that when he sensed we were creeped out by the night creatures he would say something like, "I heard that there's been some mean old bears out here." Then he'd stop like he heard one and said, "Do you hear anything?" Well, by the end of this hike, Buck and I were so close to him we were almost climbing on his back. He must have gotten a big kick out of that.

Bobo had a tattoo on his forearm that said, "Bobo" with a curved line underneath it, if I remember correctly. I was fascinated by it as in those days, not many people had them. Mostly, just military guys. Bobo got his in the Army. For many years longer than I care to admit, Bobo had a running gag going with me that I was *required by law* to get a tattoo when I turned 21. He told me it really hurt a lot and he hated the pain. I think it was Auntie Annette who finally told him to knock it off as he was scaring me. That's Bobo!

My favorite memory of the 1991 Halloween snowstorm involves Bobo. He was tending bar at the Roosevelt that night and I, living my last year in Eveleth, was also tending bar at the Roosevelt and substitute teaching. I had walked down to the bar to hang out a bit and have a drink while chatting with Bobo.

As the storm started in the early evening and Bobo was told to close the bar, I stuck around and helped him clean up a bit and headed for home. Now, living in the Jones Street house required about a four-minute walk or a two-minute jog to get home. By the time I left the bar, the storm had intensified greatly, the visibility was zero, and the snow had already been drifting due to the horrific winds. I tell this story often and it's absolutely true. That four-minute walk took almost an hour as I couldn't see and had to navigate the drifts, got confused, couldn't see quite where I was going but eventually made it, exhausted, wet, cold, and glad to be home safely. (I was probably wearing a jean jacket or light fall coat and no hat and gloves.) I hate winter clothing. If I had taken a four-minute walk to the bar, I was underdressed. For sure. (Like we knew in 1991 what weather was coming.)

Bobo, meanwhile, had driven to the bar and was attempting to drive home. Annette called and said he had phoned and said he was leaving the bar as he was closing it. Time went by, and Annette, worried, called my mom saying he hadn't come home. I think about an hour had passed. Now, in this storm, you couldn't just leave and go out and look for him. Driving was impossible. There were no cell phones, of course, to call and see what was taking him. Finally, just when Annette and my mom were almost worried enough to call the police, Bobo got home and he had a whopper of a story. He had gotten into his vehicle and attempted to drive home. It was hard going and he could not make it. He got his vehicle stuck. He ended up, if I remember right, down where lower Van Buren connects with Fayal Avenue on the way out of town. He figured he could walk the rest of the way but the wind and visibility were nada so it was impossible to navigate. He found shelter under a pine tree as he could not see well enough to go back to his vehicle and wait it out. Luckily, a passing snowmobiler came by, Bobo flagged him down, and he got a ride up Van Buren and home to a very worried Annette. She was so pissed at him, I heard, that she didn't talk to him for days. Looking back, Bobo spent 18 months in the army in Alaska so I'm sure he was used to this kind of weather and how to survive in it.

Bobo was an incredible athlete, an all-state hockey player and also baseball player, football player, and he ran track. Yes, baseball and track were during the same season and Bobo was part of the Eveleth team that ran the 400 relay at the state track meet in 1953 or 54. Anchoring that relay team was the "fastest man on land or water" Jack Ferrazzi, who ran and placed in the 100 and 220 yard dash and the 100 yard freestyle in the same year.

The best story surrounding the state relay race was that the Eveleth team, in an earlier heat, far ahead after the first baton handoff or two, dropped the baton and allowed another team to win. They were a favored team and greatly disappointed to mess up their chance. But, the story doesn't end there. Later, the team got a hold of a case of beer, and being unable to carry it into the hotel lobby, lobbed each of the 24 bottles up to a second or third floor window of the hotel where a teammate was there to catch them.

"We never dropped any of the beers," Bobo told me. "Not one."

63. What's This "Side Hustle" Crap?

It's recently come to my attention that a new phrase has been created called a "side hustle." Evidently, it means a side job or a second way to make money to supplement your income. With the creation of Uber, Lyft, Door dash, etc. people can earn extra money outside of their normal working hours.

Ok, let's think about that. Is this really new to Eveleth or Iron Range people? Really? Didn't our fathers all have two jobs or at least a second workable way to earn cash if they needed? My dad *always* had a side hustle. He was a teacher. He needed it. He tended bar, drove a Hamm's beer truck, sold pull tabs, managed the Elk's Club Bar, etc. He worked two jobs pretty much his whole working career. I think it finally ended when he was in his mid 50's and quit the job as the Elk's bar manager.

     My uncles all had side jobs. Bobo coached and tended bar. That's two side jobs. My Uncle Bill was on the chain gang at Albert Lea High School football games for like 50 years, even long after he had "retired." Demo tended bar and coached basketball along with teaching. My sister, Peg, has had her second job for almost 25 years working for a catering company in St. Cloud to go along with her job as a Spanish teacher in Milaca, MN. She's still there but now manages her own crew. She uses this job to supplement her teaching income. Her husband, my brother-in-law Tom, has coached several sports, and still is an official at track meets in Foley, MN. He also has been on a summer crew building pole barns for decades.

When I started my first teaching job in 1992, it was a forgone conclusion that I'd work a second job. I started by tending bar for Figgy Ritacco when he was Director of Catering at D'Amico Restaurant Company. I loved it and it had its benefits. I often could take extra beer or wine if the family or companies who hosted the parties didn't want it. I worked there a year and don't think I had to buy beer the whole time. After that first year, I wanted a golf job to supplement my golf habit so, as mentioned earlier, I got a golf course job in Edina thanks to Steve "Tuna" Taft and worked at it for ten golf seasons while taking advantage of hundreds of free rounds of golf at Braemar Golf Course in Edina.

So, what I'm getting at is Eveleth people (and other Iron Rangers) have always known how to "side hustle" and had the ability to earn the extra money they needed. Remember, an Iron Ranger loves to work. It's how we were raised. It's one of many things that make Iron Rangers great.

64. Who Are We, Robert Conrad?

About twenty years ago my sister Peg bought me a cool CD of other artists' versions of Bob Dylan songs. It was really cool but the best thing about it was on the back of the CD was a quote from someone else (some writer or critic) who described the Iron Range and Iron Rangers in an awesome quote:

"It's an area characterized by cold winters, blue collar struggle, and hard-nosed determination." They are famous for their tenacious intelligence, and for the chip on their shoulder."

I loved and remembered the "chip on your shoulder" part. I thought of the Robert Conrad commercial for batteries or whatever. But, what does "chip on your shoulder" mean? It's kind of negative and everyone up north then was very nice. Being arrogant in Eveleth got you punched out or ostracized. Especially in sports. So that's not it.

I think it means Iron Rangers have their ideals and the things that make them happy. They don't give a crap about what other people have and do because they get it. They get the meaning of life. They hold each other to a higher standard. They always have. You need a strong backbone to be raised in Eveleth. Physically and morally. Think about how many Evelethians over the decade were examples of this. People who were neighbors, relatives, friends' dads, coaches, teachers, etc. They were all mentors in one way or another. They had no reservations about telling you how tough life is, how important hard work is, how to treat people fairly and equally. They didn't just tell you. They showed you by example. Every time. But they showed you how to have fun and enjoy life and each other too. I still use the lessons and skills I learned in Eveleth and many of the stories I tell my students have a lesson or moral based on what was learned in Eveleth.

65. The Iron Range Attitude in Malibu?

What is that "Iron Range Attitude?" It might not stand out as much on the Range but if you move elsewhere, you might stand out. It's not in any way negative, of course. Rangers and Eveleth people in particular are always helpful, honest, hardworking, etc. We know that. But there are some things we just don't and won't change regardless of where we live or whom we meet.

I still am the most comfortable in old jeans and a beer tee shirt. Preferably Hamm's Beer, of course. I think I must have at least six or seven beer-themed shirts. My folks are always good for a new one at Christmas. When playing golf at my home course, Edinburgh USA, there is kind of a dress-code, although not real closely enforced. I don't like to rock the boat there and will wear a collared golf shirt and decent shorts when playing. I'd rather play in a beer tee shirt (or no shirt at all like we used to in Eveleth) and a pair of torn shorts or cutoff jeans.

Probably the best story of refusing to let go of your Range roots is my favorite Iron Ranger, Bob

Dylan. As stated earlier, Bob left home at 18 and never really returned other than for short visits. His main home for many years has been in Malibu, California. My wife's cousin David's son, Josh, went to Pepperdine University which is right in Malibu. He still lives there and works for a surfing company. I've known him since he was about 6 or 7 years old. He's now probably 32 or so. I used to see him every Thanksgiving but now haven't for years. My wife Traci and I got married in his parents' house in Deephaven in 1996. Josh was just a kid then.

    I've always asked if he'd seen "Bob" around. Josh and his dad are both big Dylan fans, by the way. Josh would always say anyone he knew at school or in Malibu knew when Dylan was in town. His main method of transportation was not a fancy shiny sports car but rather, an old rusted pickup truck in which there would be a dog or two in the truck bed. Kind of a very strange sight in a place like Malibu, CA especially for a singer-songwriter worth north of a couple hundred million dollars. But there you go, that old Iron Range attitude. He could afford any car he wanted but the pickup truck was more his style.

Again, making a spectacle of himself was not part of Bob's plan. He always tries to blend and be a regular guy from northern Minnesota. I'm just not sure that pickup would help him "blend" in that part of the world. I just can't imagine Neil Diamond racing around in an old pickup, though.

66. Foods Define a Culture

Not long ago I was teaching my third graders a reading unit that discussed the different ways one would define a culture. There were the obvious ones: music, dress, food, holidays, traditions, etc. I shared with them information about my ancestors and what things I learned from them that were cultural. I talked about the polka music and even went on to YouTube and played a few polka songs. Many laughed and thought it was strange. Some actually thought it was pretty cool. We talked about the foods such as polish sausage, pasties, sarmas, etc. They were very confused as I tried to explain what these foods were like. It stuck me how important it was that these cultural things needed to be introduced to young people so these ideas don't die off and become forgotten.

    I told them I thought I had done my part with my family. My three daughters have had their share of Iron Range delicacies. Their favorite is black sausage but I prefer its given name: Blood sausage. Oh yes, they know where it came from and what it's made out of and they still love it. My mom gets it from Kosher's in Gilbert or at Paul's Market. It still is wonderful and we love it. I still cook it like I always have, slowly in the oven in a pan with a bit of oil. It's done when the skin becomes a bit crispy. I cut it open like I'm performing surgery and squeeze a nice amount of yellow mustard on it.

    My wife Traci, a native of Brooklyn Center, Minnesota, just a few minutes from where we now live in Brooklyn Park, is not completely clueless about Iron Range food. She knew what a pasty was and had been eating them for many years. She doesn't like the blood sausage (probably grossed out by the name) but prefers a nice ring of potato sausage which I guess is somewhat similar. Her parents used to go to the iconic Minneapolis deli called Kramarczuk's and had their share of sausages, deli meats, and other old school foods that were similar to what was found in the Iron Range markets of old. Her family also loved porketta sandwiches when I was able to get porketta for them from "Up North."

All in all, it's important to carry on these important things that define the culture we love.

67. Those Crazy Wolf Brothers

I'm pretty sure there is a pop group called the Wolf Brothers but I'm sure I knew the first "Wolf Brothers." Now the spelling might be "Wolff" or something but I won't get caught up in the specifics.

About five houses down from 608 Jones Street toward Grant Avenue lived the Wolf(f) family. If memory serves me right, the dad was Harvey and there were two brothers and possibly a sister whose names I can't recall. The two brothers looked like the Allman Brothers, Greg and Duane. The same long hair, motorcycles, jean jackets, bad attitude, and propensity for gratuitous violence. I knew early on to keep my eyes open when walking or biking past their house.

One day I was on my bike. I must have been five years old. I was probably headed downtown to pick up Prim Skumatz's medication. When passing their house, I was suddenly hit on the left hand with an unidentified flying object. It was a large rusted bolt with an attached nut. It might have been a small trailer hitch or a part for one. It was fairly large and heavy. It opened up a decent cut near my thumb and it started bleeding just a bit. I stopped the bike to take a look at my hand and gave quick a glance toward the Wolf house. Sure enough, the brothers were in the midst of an argument on the porch. My guess is they were in their mid 20's. One of them, the older one, ran out to me and checked my hand while asking if I was ok. I was. A small cut with a bit of blood is nothing to an Eveleth kid but he seemed concerned and nice about it. It seems his crazy younger brother meant to throw it at his older brother but missed and it hit me just as I happened to cruise by on my Schwinn. I still remember the crazy eyes the younger one had as he was still angry. The nice one, while glancing back at little brother with a look that said he was about to get beaten, made sure one last time if I was fine and I took off toward main street. The last thing I heard was the loud yelling restarting as the argument continued and I was secretly hoping the younger brother was going to get his ass kicked.

68. Grandpa Tony vs. the Lawnmower

I never fail to think of this story as I mow my lawn. It comes back to me every single time. I must have been about four or five years old. I saw my Grandfather Tony Boben every day. He came to our house for coffee every morning and often stopped a second time if he knew my mom was home from work or off for the day.

It was summer and a very warm day. I was playing in my blow-up swimming pool in the back yard. Grandpa Tony came walking down the sidewalk to the back door of the Jones Street house.

He saw me and, like I did a thousand times before, I yelled out, "Hey Grandpa!"

He looked at me, didn't smile, or say a word. He bounded up the back steps and into the house. I thought it was weird that he didn't come over and tell me a joke or ask me a question or even acknowledge that I greeted him. This was not like him but I gave it little thought and went back to playing in the water.

I didn't really notice that he had a towel wrapped around his hand and wrist while his other hand gripped and held the towel in place. But it soon became apparent why.

As my mom told the family later, he came into the kitchen and she was surprised to see him as if he was coming over in the afternoon, he had a reason to. Seldom did he arrive and she wasn't expecting him. I, of course, being a curious and precocious child, followed him inside.

"Dad, what's going on, what's with the towel?" Mom asked.

"Um, I had a bit of an accident while mowing the lawn," came his reply.

"Did you cut yourself?" Now mom looked worried.

"A little worse than that...." he mumbled.

He carefully opened the towel that covered his hand and showed my mom two bloody stumps where there were fingers and two blood covered fingers completely detached from the hand they belonged to. He had stuck his hand under the edge of the mower base to clear the grass and the very edge of the whirling blades took the index and middle finger of his hand off cleanly. Luckily, I was just inside the doorway and did not see the damage.

Now, most normal people would have screamed, fainted, vomited, or turned white. Not Shirley the nurse. She was calm as to not get him agitated. Mom told me to stay in the yard or house and don't go anywhere. They went to Grandpa's truck, mom jumped in the driver's seat and they went to the Eveleth hospital. I saw Grandpa a couple of days later and his hand was still wrapped up in gauze and tape. A few days later, I got to see his fingers and they looked pretty good, the stiches still visible. Grandpa told me later that he didn't quite have all the feeling back in the fingers but he was glad they were again part of his hand. He was one tough Bohunk.

69. The Evolution of Beers in Eveleth

Over the many years of drinking and serving beers in the Eveleth bars gave me the chance to see what I call the "Evolution of Beers." It's weird that, years ago, the beers we drank and the ones that were popular in town changed. Now, Hamm's has a long history with John Karakas and his warehouse. I don't believe that will ever change even if the warehouse has long been closed. I can remember a few brands that were immensely popular then kind of died out as something new came along. When I became a legal bar drinker in July of 1985, it seems that you couldn't look anywhere without seeing a Special Export Light bottle. It must have outsold everything else twofold. Those green bottles were always on the bar and it seemed that nothing else was ordered. As a bartender at the Roosevelt, we always had a good idea what was popular and what was moving. We had to have Hamm's of course. The long neck returnable bottles were popular then. I can remember a few guys drank Pabst. If you drank a "Blue Ribbon," you probably didn't ever drink Hamm's as we looked at those two as competitors. I think they might now be distributed together as I think Pabst now owns Hamm's. Interestingly, both Pabst and Hamm's are now considered "hipster" beers in the Twin Cities, especially in "Nordeast" Minneapolis with its ample supply of dive bars. I've actually kind of developed a fondness for Pabst if I see it on a drink menu and will occasionally order one.

You can also see Hamm's at a few select bars and restaurants in the Twin Cities but mostly because of some kind of Iron Range connection. Craig "Figgy" Ritacco carries it at the place he runs, "The Lexington" on Grand Avenue in St. Paul. Across the street from the Lex is the Iron Range Grille, owned by Tom Forti of Hibbing, MN. Tom also has one of the cool Hamm's signs with the moving water behind his cool little bar. Joe Bennett, originally from Mountain Iron, also carries Hamm's at his place, Bennett's Chop and Rail House, on West 7th in St. Paul. Old habits never die.

 I was thrilled that my home bar, The Brooklyn at Edinburgh USA Golf Course, recently started carrying 16oz. Hamm's cans since one of the teaching pros liked it. Then, just as abruptly, they claimed they couldn't get it and it was gone, even though it was a pretty good seller. I think that was an excuse as you could easily pick up a 36 pack at the local liquor store. I think they dropped it to make room for the most popular of watered-down crap beers, Coors Light. With all the craft beer available now, it's hard to believe that Coors Light is so popular. Don't even get me started on Bud Light or Miller Light. I always look at those as beers for people who don't actually like beer.

I remember when Old Style was a popular tap beer in Eveleth. The Roosevelt also carried Blatz, Schmidt, Old Style, and Budweiser, along with Hamm's and Pabst in returnable bottles. I don't ever remember popping the cap on a Coors Light for anyone! There might have been a couple more brands but they were not that popular. Currently, the craze is those seltzers that you see everywhere. They remind me of Zima, which had a short run in the 80's. My good friend, Mike "Who? Hals" Hallstrom loves his White Claw seltzers. I think they call them "Clams" in Eveleth. Yuck. I think I'll just stick to vodka.

70. Those Damned Tusa Twins

I know I've written quite a bit about the crazy twins on Golf Course Road but heck, they give us plenty of material.

I recently got reacquainted with Keith and Kevan Tusa and we started fishing together occasionally. We fished quite a bit while in high school and it's been fun to spend time in a boat with them telling stories and talking about those days 40 years ago.

But things have changed: We used to fit three of us in the boys' 8-foot canoe catching crappies by the dozens in St. Mary's Lake. We rarely wanted to spend any money on fancy tackle or bait. I remember catching crappies on bubblegum. Or we took a rubber twister tail and broke it into pieces to use as bait. The many crappies in St. Mary's must be blind and/or stupid as we always caught a bunch on whatever we threw at them. Now, it's different. Keith and Kevan both have their own boats and a lot of the fancy equipment and technology. I always say my favorite kind of boat is "someone else's." We don't have to cruise the lake looking for the crappies by dropping lines everywhere. The cool fish finder Keith has made this part easier. We can cruise around looking for the right spot and the right lake structure by looking at his screen. Large schools of crappies also can show up on the screen. It's pretty cool and way different than the guessing game we played in the early 1980's. One thing stays the same: We still love crappie fishing.

71. No Study Hall for Hilf

My good friend from high school, Tommy Hilfers, was a piece of work. He just could not get up early enough for his first hour class. Never. I don't think he ever made it to his first hour class, which I believe was study hall.

In the spring, when our graduation pictures came out and we spent a ton of time sharing pictures with classmates, Mike Hallstrom and I decided to do something really funny. We both had our own grad pictures that Hilf had given us. We walked into the main office and the principal's secretary, Laura Maki, was sitting at her desk. We had this idea that we'd use Hilf's grad picture and make "Missing Posters" to display in the hallway, on lockers, etc. But we needed Laura's help. Luckily, she liked us. After politely asking her if we could use the office copy machine and she asked if it was copies for a teacher or just for us.

"We're making a missing poster with Hilf's picture on it as a joke," Laura was well aware that Hilf was late to first hour every single day.

She smirked and said "Ok, but don't tell the man I let you." The man, of course, was Principal Melgeorge and we were very nervous about getting caught.

Mike was a great artist so we copied just one of Hilf's pictures, blown up slightly, onto the upper corner of the paper. Mike, with his steady drawing hand, made a cool poster with cool lettering on the paper. It said, "Missing from First Hour Study Hall" and a physical description and a warning to not approach him as he could be dangerous. When it was finished, it looked great. We ran excitedly back to the office and made like 50 copies of it. We borrowed Laura's tape dispenser and we were off and running. School let out a few minutes before so Mike and I were not seen by many as we taped up the 50 copies of the poster on lockers, walls, and tacked a few of them onto bulletin boards, etc.

    The next morning, Hilf was absent again until 9am. We saw him walk in and it didn't take long for him to see the posters. He thought it was great and took one to put inside his locker. It was a great laugh but I'm assuming Principal Melgeorge didn't find it funny and had the custodial staff take them down at the end of the day. I don't remember if he ever found out who did it.

72. What the Hell is Sloe Gin?

I'll go to my grave with no answer to this question. This is from a renowned liquor enthusiast from both sides of the bar. I've got a history with this shit.

(As a side note, I've also enjoyed a bottle of absinthe, the hallucinatory liquor which is 150 proof, and which just became legal in the US in the past decade.) It's said that Vincent van Gogh drank a bunch of it to deaden the pain before cutting his own ear off.)

Ok, my drinking history or what I enjoyed to drink has been a very hilly ride. For the first few years of the drinking career, I could not just settle in on a favorite beer or liquor, and never really developing a taste for either. So, I had a short dance with that rotten shit called Sloe Gin. I think I usually mixed it with 7up or Sprite. I think it must have started during the cold months where one idea was drinking inside the movie theater. It seemed too good to be true! Bring in a half pint of liquor and buy a large movie theater soda. Drink a third of the soda as you demolish handfuls of popcorn, pour the half pint into the soda cup, lean back, stretch out your legs, and enjoy the show. We did it a few times. By the time the weather got warmer, it was drinking outside or in the woods somewhere so the whole thing was a short-lived idea. We stopped it before we got caught. I don't know if was the falling asleep during the movie, too many trips to the bathroom or the time someone set down their empty half pint, it tipped and *clink clink clinked* its way down the high to low concrete floor beneath us while we laughed our asses off. God, we could be assholes. I also remember drinking that crap in the spring time which was great as we could start cruising Chestnut Street in Virginia after getting buzzed up outside somewhere nearby. A personal favorite was the old train car that was at the end of Chestnut Street. I think it was just abandoned and bums slept in it. There also were train cars usually just sitting on the towns' edge to the right of the M & H Gas Station off of Second Avenue. I know we sat under those drinking out of paper bags to play the part of hobos more than once.

73. R. John and Shirley

I'm immensely proud of my upbringing in Eveleth and honored to be the first born of John and Shirley. I was raised with just the right amount of love and also the right amount of ass kicking when I deserved it. I was blessed to live during a good time in Eveleth. So many adults in town were my mentors and kept an eye out for me when needed. So many of the characters were still around. I feel sorry for kids nowadays. There is not as much freedom to be a kid. There are too many bad people out there, and kids' lives are too busy and scripted. They spend too much time at home with their parents so they can't develop as many skills on their own or learn to navigate this difficult world. As a teacher, I see students who lack confidence or the ability to solve their own problems because parents solve every problem for their kids.

By the time I was eight years old, I was making my own money through odd jobs and had a paper route. I had seen the inside of quite a few Iron Range bars and experienced things kids today could not comprehend or understand. I hitchhiked a few times before I was 15, spent time wandering the woods with a shotgun when I was 10 or 11, once put an ice pick all the way through my hand while punching holes in a jar for some stupid caterpillar I found. (No sympathy from Shirley.) I bought cigarettes and prescription meds for my grandfather and Prim Skumatz. I jumped bikes over rows of garbage cans and climbed trees that were 50 feet tall. I grabbed onto bumpers of cars in the winter for free rides and in the summer, jumped off 60-foot cliffs into mine pit lakes hundreds of feet deep. I fist fought and wrestled, bloodied my knees and elbows from bike accidents, and cut myself playing with knives too many times to count. I must have had 50 stitches put into my body and I took out *every one* by myself to prove I could do it. Except the ones in my scalp from Christmas Eve 1982.

I could cook by the time I was 7 or 8 and was raised by a tough woman who told me, "No woman is ever going to need to take care of *my* son." I could cook, clean, do laundry, and take care of myself at a very young age. Shirley would have been horrified if I needed a wife to cook or clean up after me. My parents taught me to always take care of others and not to be a burden to anyone. They taught me to treat everyone equally and that respect is earned.

My parents proudly voted against limiting marriage to only heterosexual couples in 2011, as did I. Shirley said, "We are all God's children." I couldn't have been prouder. My parents have put in thousands of hours of volunteering to help their community, their friends, their neighbors, and even strangers but are themselves too proud to accept much help from others. Shirley has spent decades cutting newspaper clippings from the local papers to send to classmates living far away so they can keep up with the news in Eveleth. Mom and Dad have spent hundreds of hours over many years visiting people in the nursing home. Some they knew, others were just people who needed company. They've lived their lives in service to others like they were taught in church. They walk the walk, every single day and I couldn't have been raised by better humans. I try hard to live my life in a way that makes them proud. I probably come up well short of what John and Shirley accomplish each day but I always try my best. My sister and I are very very lucky and, as we have aged, we realize how blessed we were.

74. It's 2023: We're Still Here

Alright, this book project has been hanging over my head for too long. It's like a school project that I have a nightmare about because I lost it or forgot to turn it in.

A lot has happened since this book was started. My uncles Demo Mayasich and Bobo Kochevar are gone, as is Pat Forte, Doc Martinson, and my high school golf coach Bill McKenzie. It's post COVID-19 and the world has become a veritable shit show. But, we've survived to live another day.

I'm currently 56 years old and will turn 57 this year (2023). I'm a senior citizen but don't feel like it. My girls, just teenagers when this project was started, are now 24(Jamie) and 20(Jenna and Lauren.) I'm immensely proud of them. They are in college and working hard, two jobs each sometimes. They currently work at my "home away from home" The Brooklyn Bar and Restaurant at Edinburgh USA, my home golf course, just about a 500-yard walk from our backyard. They also work as nannies and have learned valuable lessons while raising babies and toddlers. They'll make terrific mothers if they choose to someday. They know how to "hustle" money like R. John used to say.

My wife Traci and I will have been married 26 years on September 27, 2022. Traci should, by now, have earned her purple heart. Like my mom once said, "Being married to you must be tough."

Time flies. I've been teaching for 32 years, with probably at least six more to go before I can afford to retire. I have no plans to sit on a beach or rocking chair anytime soon. I will probably go to work at Edinburgh too, my preference would be early morning grounds crew work, riding a mower, changing tees and cups, whatever. I began my work career as a 13-year-old at the Eveleth Golf Course. I might as well end it like that at Edinburgh.

    Thank you for reading. Be good to each other. Peace.

Tom Intihar
February 2023

Lists

In his memoir, Ed Weir from Virginia made a list of his favorite books to encourage others to read them. I'll do him one better and add mine *and* a list of my favorite albums:

Books

In Cold Blood by Truman Capote (1966) I read it in college for an English class but didn't realize just how good or groundbreaking it was until I reread it much later. Capote called it a "nonfiction novel." The movie *Capote (2005)* with Philiip Seymour Hoffman is all about this book and crime.

Junky by William S. Burroughs. (1953) Burroughs' alter ego, William Lee, is the title character. It's basically a memoir but it was the

1950's, so you didn't go around advertising you were a hopeless junkie.

On the Road by Jack Kerouac (1957) I know this book is cliché but it is really good. You get lost in it. The original typed manuscript was many pages taped together in a scroll 120 feet long and typed almost nonstop in 20 days of coffee and amphetamine-fueled typing sessions. It still sells 60,000 copies a year. The scroll is now owned by Indianapolis Colts owner Jim Irsay who had it restored and it now tours the country to be seen by interested Beat Generation fans. I've owned three copies of this book and usually just give them away.

Chronicles Volume 1 by Bob Dylan (2004) A memoir of his early years in New York City.

Heavier than Heaven by Charles R. Cross (2001) A biography of Kurt Cobain; the best rock star biography I've ever read, period. He was an unbelievable talent whose genius was not fully realized until years after he committed suicide in 1994. He idolized the Beatles. He might not have started grunge music, but he gave it melody.

Golf Monster by Alice Cooper (2007) A great bio with alternating chapters about his life in music and his love of golf.   He could really play golf too!

Acid for the Children by Flea (Michael Balzary)(2019) A memoir by the bassist for the Red Hot Chili Peppers. I think the plan was to write about his life from birth to present but he had like 300 pages written by the time he got to when the Peppers first got big. His formative years were really strange.

Nights in White Castle Steve Rushin (2019) A memoir of growing up in Bloomington, MN by a

1984 graduate of Kennedy High School. He could have hung out with our group in Eveleth. Very funny book!

<u>Truer Than Strange</u> by Ray Reigstad (2011) Written by a 1984 Eveleth High School graduate and one of the models for my book. It's so fun reading about people you know.

Albums

(I've owned hundreds but probably played these more than any others)

The Times They are A-Changing: Bob Dylan (1964)

Rubber Soul: The Beatles (1965)

Bringing it All Back Home: Bob Dylan (1965)

Blond on Blond: Bob Dylan (1966)

Pet Sounds: The Beach Boys (1966)

Beggar's Banquet: The Rolling Stones (1968)

Crosby, Stills, and Nash: Crosby, Stills, and Nash (1969)

Let it Bleed: The Rolling Stones (1969)

Abbey Road: The Beatles (1969)

The Guilded Palace of Sin: The Flying Burrito Brothers (1969)

Tapestry: Carole King (1971)

Harvest: Neil Young (1972)

GP: Gram Parsons (1973)

Live at the Old Quarter: Townes Van Zandt (1973)

Blood on the Tracks: Bob Dylan (1975)

Born to Run: Bruce Springsteen (1975)

Murmur: REM (1983)

Fables of the Reconstruction: REM (1984)

The Early Years: Part One and Two: Tom Waits (1991, 93)

Hollywood Town Hall: The Jayhawks (1992)

Harvest Moon: Neil Young (1992)

Brood: The Glenrustles (1995)

Stranger's Almanac: Whiskeytown (1997)

Sky Blue Sky: Wilco (2007)

Townes: Steve Earle (2009)

A special thanks to my good buddy, Michael "Mick" Maki who taught me about Bob Dylan, Gram Parsons, Towns Van Zandt, and the restorative power of listening to good songwriting. I cherish your friendship Mick.

Many thanks to Ellen Johnson for the cover design of this book and other techie stuff I'm too old to know and do myself. These kids know everything.

Made in the USA
Monee, IL
09 March 2023

29538503R00144